Air Fryer R

150+ YUMMY AIR FRYER RECIPES

Get more support at AirFryerChallenge.com

Find my favorite accessories at AirFryerTools.com

CONTENTS

HI FRIEND!

My name is **Cathy Yoder**. I am a mother of 8 kids, a wife to my hubby since 1994, and the owner and **CEO of FabulesslyFrugal.com** since 2008. And I LOVE helping people!

On my website, I have a team of women who scour the internet for the best deals around. I also have lots of recipes and DIY tips and tricks. In 2020 I decided to focus on YouTube and help people actually USE the air fryer they've purchased.

Let's face it, new appliances can be overwhelming, so my hope is this cookbook will give you confidence to go beyond the air fryer basics and really uplevel what you make in your air fryer.

Anyone that knows me knows that I am not a fan of complicated recipes and crazy ingredients. So rest assured, these recipes are simple enough for practically anyone to make!

If you haven't seen me on YouTube yet, search for "*air fryer recipes*" on YouTube and you'll see a video with my face on it! I also share tips and tricks and all you need to know about your air fryer.

And I have so much gratitude to express, because there is no way I could do all I do, without the help of so many!

First, I give thanks and acknowledge a loving Heavenly Father and His son, Jesus Christ, who empower me to do more than I ever dreamed I was capable of. I am so blessed to know I am a daughter of God!

Thanks to my team at **FabulesslyFrugal.com**, who tolerate my messages when I am seeking feedback and opinions. Thanks to my team of talented photographers, Melanie, Sarah, Katie, Karen and Amanda, who make food look much better than I ever could. Thanks to **Kristen from SixSistersStuff**, who shared her time with me 3 days before Christmas in 2019 and convinced me to hop on YouTube. Thanks to my viewers and readers who kindly share gratitude and kind words, their experiences and stories. These messages often come at the end of long tiring days and remind me that my work in the world matters. Thanks to viewer Lynne, from Canada, who was brave enough to send me an email critiquing my first e-book. Little did she know 5 months later I would hire her to edit my first cookbook! Thanks to my business partner and friend, BJ, for encouraging me and helping me stay focused and sane through all the big projects I dive into. Thanks to my sweet friends who help fill in the gaps and are second mothers to my children. Thanks to my wonderful parents and 5 siblings for helping me be the person I am today and for always being my cheerleaders. And lastly, thanks to my **husband Roman**, who has stood next to me, through thick and thin, and has supported me through this crazy ride of being a business owner. And to our 8 beautiful children, thanks for being my ultimate taste testers. But more importantly for letting me be your mama. I am the luckiest girl.

And thank YOU, my new friend, for allowing me into your home and kitchen. I hope this book helps you unlock all the fun your air fryer has to offer and makes your life just a little bit easier.

Best,

Cathy Yoder

This cookbook is sorted into six sections: Breakfast, Main Dishes (grouped by protein), Veggies & Sides, Snack & Sandwiches, and Desserts! Then at the end of the book you'll find some more quick tips, cheat sheets, conversion charts and more! The index has been arranged to help you quickly find recipes in different categories and ingredients. As you are planning your meals, see what you already have in the fridge and pantry and use it up!

Then mark up the cookbook! Jot down notes to remind you what times worked best for your air fryer and what changes you would make next time (if any). If you don't like a certain veggie or seasoning in a recipe, swap it out for something you do like! Have fun with it!

And remember, since every brand of air fryer is slightly different (namely size and wattage), you may have to make minor adjustments to the timing. My air fryer is a 1700 watt 5.8 quart Cosori© Air Fryer, so these times & temps are centered around that. If your air fryer is a lower watt air fryer, you may need to add a few extra minutes of cook time. The same holds true if you have a large oven style air fryer. Food may take longer to cook because it's not compact like a basket style air fryer.

However, I have GOOD NEWS! Since it's so easy to check on the food while it's cooking, it won't take long for you to learn how your air fryer cooks and what adjustments you will need to make (if any at all).

Let's Talk About Safety:

The first rules of any kitchen should be SAFETY FIRST, SAFETY SECOND and SAFETY THIRD!!

An air fryer is a very handy addition to any kitchen making any cook's life easier. But basic safety must be followed. Many people start using appliances without ever reading the safety section of the manual.

An air fryer blows hot air out through a vent in the back, which can damage the surrounding walls and your overhead cupboards. So when in use, always place it on a heat-safe surface and make sure there is adequate room around it on all sides and overhead.

Never place your air fryer on top of your stove! If it accidentally gets turned on you can destroy your air fryer but the stove surface can also be damaged past repair.

Use oven mitts, silicone tongs and other heat-safe items to remove food or containers from the air fryer. Make sure you have a heat-proof surface nearby to place the hot basket or dish on. Have a wooden cutting board, trivet or silicone pad on your counter ready for both the bottom section and the basket.

Do not use plastic dishes in your air fryer. Only use oven-safe dishes that can withstand up to 450°F/232°C. Do not use metal or anything that will scratch the coating in your air fryer. Take care of your air fryer and it will take care of you!

20 Air Fryer Tips & Tricks

BEFORE YOU AIR FRY

1. **Make sure the air fryer is clean and empty.** Need I say more?

2. **Never preheat the air fryer with parchment paper inside.** It will blow up into the heating element and start to burn. When you do use parchment paper (I like to use it for those times I'm cooking extra messy foods). Just be sure the food holds the parchment paper down so it doesn't fly up into the burner. You can also set a small wire rack on top of the food (see AirFryerTools.com for links to items like this).

3. **Line underneath the air fryer basket with foil for quick and easy clean up.**

4. **Parboil root vegetables before cooking them in the air fryer.** Then use the air fryer to finish roasting the vegetables to save time.

5. **Get creative with your seasonings on your proteins.** Wet marinades and dry rubs work great in the air fryer!

WHILE YOU ARE AIR FRYING

6. **Start small.** Start testing out your air fryer by cooking less expensive foods. If you mess up a batch, you don't break the bank! A few of my favorite foods to start with are frozen hamburger patties, chicken wings, and frozen broccoli.

7. **Open the air fryer.** The air fryer is small and compact, which makes checking on the progress of your food a lot easier. Open your air fryer, check on your food, and make adjustments as needed. Most air fryers will pause when you open them. If not, look for a pause button.

8. **Use an instant read food thermometer.** Sometimes it will be enough to look at your food and know if it is done or not. However, for most foods, you will need to use an instant read food thermometer to gauge whether your food has finished cooking or not. See the temperature guide at the back of this book and you'll always know what the internal temp of meats and baked goods should be! Get my favorite instant read meat thermometer at AirFryerTools.com.

9. **Never ever set your air fryer on the stove.** If your stove accidentally gets turned and your air fryer is also on your stove, not only is your air fryer toast, but so is your stove! Just don't do it!

10. **Use a reusable oil sprayer.** Most commercial oil sprays you buy at the store are full of propellants and chemicals that will ruin your basket. Instead, use a spray bottle and fill it with your own healthy oil that has a high smoke point! In the long run, it saves money! I always use avocado oil and you'll find my favorite oil sprayer at **AirFryerTools.com**.

11. **Use water or bread to keep the air fryer from smoking.** If you're cooking fatty foods such as bacon or sausage in the air fryer, put either a ¼ cup of water or a slice of bread in the base of the air fryer to absorb grease.

12. **Use a wire rack to keep foods from flying around in the air fryer basket** (see AirFryerTools. com).

13. **Let cheese melt in a hot air fryer.** Viewer Sandy shared this great tip for adding melted cheese to a burger: when the burger is done cooking, add the cheese, then close the air fryer door. Let it sit for about a minute or so and not only does it melt perfectly, but it never slides off too!

14. **Make a foil sling for foods that are hard to take out of the air fryer basket.** Just make sure you leave room along the sides for air flow! Simply make a large rectangle with handles that you set delicate foods on. That way you can just lift the foil (and the food) out of the air fryer with ease.

15. **Reheat leftovers in the air fryer.** Revive leftovers such as fries, pizza, breaded foods, tortilla chips AND things like steak and chicken. For best results, let the food sit out, covered, for 15ish minutes. Then, preheat the air fryer at 400°F/200°C for 5 minutes. Next, place the food inside and air fry at 370°F/185°C in 3 minute increments. Rotate and cook longer as needed.

AFTER USING YOUR AIR FRYER

16. **Clean your air fryer after each meal.** Wipe down the top and bottom of the air fryer and clean the air fryer basket. NEVER use abrasives to clean your air fryer. That will wear your air fryer basket down quickly.

17. **Use Dawn Powerwash to clean the air fryer basket.** Once the air fryer has cooled down and you've wiped out the majority of grease and food chunks, spray the basket with Dawn Powerwash don't add water, and let it sit for 10 minutes or so. Wipe it out, then wash it with hot water.

18. **Wipe down the cooled heating element with a damp paper towel.** This will help prevent build up of food splatters and grease.

19. **Use the air fryer to dry the air fryer basket.** Pop the wet air fryer basket into the air fryer and run it for a few minutes to dry the basket. Let the air fryer cool completely before putting it away.

20. **Contact your air fryer manufacturer before buying a new air fryer.** If you feel like your air fryer basket has passed the point of no return, rather than buying a whole new unit, see if your manufacturer sells just the basket replacement!

NOTES

BREAKFAST

Simple & Amazing Bacon

You'll never cook bacon any other way! Cooking bacon in an air fryer is perfection when you follow these tips. And clean up is so easy!

PREP TIME: 5 minutes   **COOK TIME:** 10 minutes   **TOTAL TIME:** 15 minutes   **SERVES:** 4

RECIPE INGREDIENTS

- 1 or 2 slices bread
- 4-8 slices bacon

RECIPE NOTES

For easy clean up, let the grease cool slightly then wipe out the air fryer basket using a paper towel, and clean as usual.

INSTRUCTIONS

01 Rip the bread slices into 4 total large pieces and place them under the air fryer basket to help catch grease drippings and prevent smoking.

02 Place bacon in basket, it is ok if the bacon overlaps in the beginning, because it will shrink while cooking.

03 Cook at 380°F/193°C for 8-10 minutes. Check halfway through cooking time seperate it and rotate it, if desired. Cooking time will vary depending on your air fryer, the thickness of your bacon, and how crisp you like it.

Ham and Cheese Breakfast Egg Rolls

Simple, but tasty – these breakfast egg rolls are always a welcome easy meal at my house.

PREP TIME: 20 minutes   **COOK TIME:** 6 minutes   **TOTAL TIME:** 26 minutes   **SERVES:** 8

RECIPE INGREDIENTS

- 12 large eggs
- salt and pepper to taste
- 1/2 cup shredded cheese
- 8 oz diced ham
- 16 egg roll wrappers
- oil spray

INSTRUCTIONS

01. Whisk eggs in a large skillet over medium heat. Season with salt and pepper. Cook, stirring often, until eggs are just cooked through. Add ham and cook for an additional 1-2 minutes. Stir in cheese and remove from heat.

02. Scoop about 1/3 cup (or 1/16th) of egg mixture onto an egg roll wrapper. Fold bottom corner up over filling, then fold side corners in (like an envelope), and roll it up (see photos in blog post or back of package for visual instructions). Dab a bit of water on the top corner before rolling all the way to help it stick. Repeat for each egg roll.

03. Spray air fryer basket with oil spray. Place 4-7 egg rolls in the basket, however many your air fryer can fit without them touching, seam-side down. Spray egg rolls with oil spray. Cook at 400°F/200°C for 6-8 minutes, until golden and crispy on the outside.

Crustless Quiche

*Enjoy this tasty, simple, and healthy crustless quiche in your air fryer.
This recipe is wonderful because you can easily adapt the contents of
the quiche with your own personal favorites!*

PREP TIME: 10 minutes   **COOK TIME:** 18 minutes   **TOTAL TIME:** 28 minutes   **SERVES:** 2

RECIPE INGREDIENTS

- 4 links sausage, remove the casing and cut into pieces
- 3 oz spinach
- 1 tbsp water
- small handful of your favorite cheese
- 1/3 c milk
- 3-4 eggs, beaten
- 1/4 tsp salt
- dash of pepper
- pinch of nutmeg

INSTRUCTIONS

01. Cook sausage in the air fryer for 3 minutes at 350°F/176°C. Flip, then cook for an additional 3 minutes at 370°F/187°C.

02. While sausage cooks, steam the spinach and water in a covered bowl for 2 minutes in the microwave. Squeeze out excess water and let cool.

03. In a bowl, whisk together the milk, eggs, salt, pepper and nutmeg.

04. Place the cooked sausage in a lightly sprayed air fryer pizza pan, top with spinach and cheese. Then pour the egg and milk mixture on top.

05. Cook at 350°F/176°C for 12 minutes or until an inserted toothpick comes out clean.

Hard "Boiled" Eggs

Why heat up the stove with boiling water? Make perfect hard boiled eggs in the air fryer.

PREP TIME: 1 minutes   **COOK TIME:** 10 minutes   **TOTAL TIME:** 11 minutes   **SERVES:** 6

RECIPE INGREDIENTS

✓ 6 large Eggs

RECIPE NOTES

You can store these in the refrigerator for up to 7 days. Depending on the size of your basket you can cook up to 10 eggs at a time.

INSTRUCTIONS

01 Add the eggs to the air fryer basket.

02 Cook at 270°F/132°C for 15 minutes for hard cooked eggs, 12-13 minutes for jammy eggs, 9-11 minutes for soft cooked eggs.

03 Immerse eggs in an ice water bath for 10 minutes. Use immediately or refrigerate.

Sausage Egg Muffin Cups

Sausage egg muffin cups are the perfect go-to breakfast item that you can make in your air fryer!

PREP TIME: 5 minutes   **COOK TIME:** 12 minutes   **TOTAL TIME:** 17 minutes   **SERVES:** 4

RECIPE INGREDIENTS

✓ 12 Johnsonville Sausage Strips™ or partially cooked bacon

✓ 1-2 slices of bread, cubed

✓ 8 large eggs

✓ sea salt

RECIPE NOTES

If using bacon, instead of Johnsonville Sausage Strips™, cook the bacon in the cups for about 4 minutes, then add the bread and egg and finish cooking.

INSTRUCTIONS

01 Line each silicone muffin cup with sausage strips to make a "nest" inside the cup. I used about one and a half slices of sausage strips for each cup. Then place silicone muffin liners in the air fryer basket.

02 Place a few pieces of cubed bread inside each cup, then crack an egg in each cup and top with salt and pepper.

03 Air fry at 340°F/170°C for 12 minutes or until eggs are baked to your liking.

Egg Bake in Minutes!

Simple, delicious, and personal egg bakes that everyone will love!

PREP TIME: 5 minutes   **COOK TIME:** 15 minutes   **TOTAL TIME:** 20 minutes   **SERVES:** 4

RECIPE INGREDIENTS

- 4 large eggs
- 2 tbsp half and half or milk, (the amount here can be whatever you prefer!)
- salt and pepper to taste

CUSTOMIZE YOUR ADD-INS. FOR EXAMPLE

- leftover potatoes, cubed
- cheese, shredded or sliced
- bacon, chopped
- chopped spinach

INSTRUCTIONS

01 Crack one egg into each of the ramekins. Add in half and half. Whisk together.

02 The best part of these air fryer egg bakes is that you can totally customize each egg to your liking. For example, I love spinach, cheese, and salt and pepper in these. Feel free to add any of your favorite egg/omelet toppings. For inspiration: leftover potatoes, bacon, bell pepper, zucchini, ham, or Italian seasoning and garlic powder.

03 Add ramekins to air fryer basket and cook for 15 minutes at 350°F/176°C. Check on the eggs 2-3 times and give each a stir with a fork or whisk.

04 Egg Bakes are done when egg mixture is set.

TOOLS:
Use 8 oz ramekins or any small oven safe dishes. Find them at AirFryerTools.com.

Breakfast Bowl

You'll love how easy it is to throw this hearty breakfast bowl together!

PREP TIME: 5 minutes   **COOK TIME:** 15 minutes   **TOTAL TIME:** 20 minutes   **SERVES:** 2-4

RECIPE INGREDIENTS

- ✓ 5-6 frozen chicken nuggets
- ✓ 10 frozen tater tots
- ✓ 4 large eggs
- ✓ 1/4 c milk
- ✓ shredded cheese, optional

TOOLS

Use a 7" air fryer "cake barrel" or any oven safe dish. Find it at AirFryerTools.com.

INSTRUCTIONS

01. Preheat the air fryer at 400°F/200°C for 5 minutes.

02. Place the chicken nuggets and tater tots in the air fryer basket and cook for 6 minutes at at 400°F/200°C.

03. Meanwhile, whisk together the eggs and milk.

04. Chop up the chicken and tots into bite sized pieces.

05. Pour the egg mixture into a lightly greased 7" cake barrel (or any air fryer safe dish). Add the chicken and tots.

06. Place the cake barrel in the air fryer basket and cook for 7 minutes at 350°F/175°C.

07. Stir the eggs and cook for an additional 3-4 minutes.

08. Top with shredded cheese and cook for 1 more minute to melt the cheese.

Breakfast Bombs

*Air fryer breakfast bombs are the bomb, to say the least! This recipe is a
great, quick and easy breakfast idea that everyone will love.*

PREP TIME: 20 minutes   **COOK TIME:** 12 minutes   **TOTAL TIME:** 32 minutes   **SERVES:** 4

RECIPE INGREDIENTS

- 1 can Grands Flaky! Biscuits
- 2 large eggs
- 4 pieces bacon
- 1 tsp butter
- 2/3 c shredded cheddar cheese

EGG WASH

- 1 egg
- 1 tbsp water

INSTRUCTIONS

01 In a medium sized skillet, cook the bacon until crispy and set aside. Drain the grease from the skillet and wipe the skillet clean.

02 Return the skillet back to the heat and add the butter to the skillet. Once the butter is melted, add the eggs and scramble them until fully cooked, but still moist. Remove from heat and set aside.

03 Crumble the bacon into the egg mixture.

04 Place a piece of air fryer parchment paper to the liner of the air fryer basket and lightly spray with oil.

05 Take each biscuit and pull it apart or cut it in half. Create a small little bowl with one half and add about a tbsp of the egg mixture. Top with the shredded cheese, and then add the top half of the biscuit. Pinch the seams together and set aside as you finish the remainder of the biscuit bombs.

06 Create the egg wash by mixing the egg and water in a small bowl. Brush the egg wash over each biscuit bomb covering them completely.

07 Place the biscuit bombs into the bottom of the air fryer basket, making sure to leave enough room around the biscuits to fully cook and receive air flow. Cook at 320°F/160°C for 8 minutes.

08 Flip the biscuit bombs in the basket and cook for an additional 2-4 minutes until the tops are golden brown and fully cooked. Serve warm!

French Toast Sticks

These French toast sticks are so sweet and crispy. Plus, when you make them in the air fryer you can get them just as crispy or soft as you want!

PREP TIME: 10 minutes   **COOK TIME:** 8 minutes   **TOTAL TIME:** 18 minutes   **SERVES:** 6

RECIPE INGREDIENTS

- 12 thick slices hearty white sandwich bread (I used Texas Toast)
- 1 1/2 c whole milk, warmed slightly
- 4 tbsp butter melted
- 3 large egg yolks
- 3-4 tbsp brown sugar
- 1/2 tsp ground cinnamon
- 1 tbsp vanilla extract

RECIPE NOTES

Thick sliced bread is key with this recipe. Otherwise regular sliced bread will result in super soggy or super crispy French toast sticks.

INSTRUCTIONS

01 Cut your bread into thirds and place sticks in a single layer in the air fryer at 350°F/176°C for 2 minutes. This will dry your bread out just enough so that you won't have soggy bread sticks.

02 While your bread is in the air fryer, make your dipping mixture.

03 Combine milk, melted butter and egg yolks with an immersion blender, fork, or whisk. (Because I used my immersion blender, I put my mixture in a 4-c measuring cup to safely mix).

04 Mix in vanilla, cinnamon, and brown sugar until sugar is dissolved.

05 Pour mixture into a shallow glass dish.

06 Grab your bread sticks, place into batter and flip around.

07 Place a single layer into air fryer leaving a bit of space around each one.

08 Sprinkle with more cinnamon and sugar if desired.

09 Cook at 350°F/176°C for 8 minutes, flipping the sticks halfway through.

10 If you want your French toast sticks crispier, cook for an extra minute or two.

11 Serve with your favorite toppings!

Raspberry French Toast Cups

Tasty, delicious, and simple French toast cups in the air fryer are the perfect treat to make anyone's morning a little extra special!

RECIPE INGREDIENTS

FRENCH TOAST CUPS

- 4 slices Italian bread, cut into 1/2-inch cubes
- 1 c fresh or frozen raspberries
- 4 ounces cream cheese, cut into 1/2-inch cubes
- 4 large eggs
- 1 c whole milk
- 2 tbsp maple syrup

RASPBERRY LEMON SYRUP

- 4 tsp cornstarch
- 2/3 c water
- 4 c fresh or frozen raspberries divided
- 2 tbsp lemon juice
- 2 tbsp maple syrup
- 1 tsp grated lemon zest
- ground cinnamon optional, to taste

INSTRUCTIONS

FRENCH TOAST CUPS

01. Cut the bread and cream cheese into 1/2 inch cubes.

02. Lightly grease 4, 8-ounce ramekins. Divide the bread cubes into 4 equals parts. Place some of the bread into each of the ramekins. Add raspberries and cream cheese. Top with remaining bread.

03. In a small bowl, whisk the eggs, milk, and syrup together. Pour over the bread. Cover and refrigerate for at least 1 hour.

04. Preheat the air fryer to 320°F/160°C for 3-5 minutes. Place ramekins in the air fryer basket. Cook for 12-15 minutes at 320°F/160°C, until golden brown and puffed.

RASPBERRY LEMON SYRUP

01. Meanwhile, in a saucepan, combine cornstarch and water until smooth.

02. Add 3 cups of the raspberries, lemon juice, syrup and lemon zest. Bring to a boil; reduce heat. Cook and stir until thickened, about 2 minutes. Strain and discard seeds; cool slightly.

03. Gently stir remaining 1 cup berries into syrup.

04. If desired, sprinkle French toast cups with cinnamon; serve with syrup.

Pancake Donuts

So tender, fluffy, and delicious! I could eat these pancake donuts everyday!

PREP TIME: 15 minutes   **COOK TIME:** 7 minutes   **TOTAL TIME:** 22 minutes   **SERVES:** 3

RECIPE INGREDIENTS

- 1 c flour
- 2 tsp sugar
- 1/2 tsp baking powder
- 1/4 tsp baking soda
- 1/3 tsp salt
- 1/2 c sour cream
- 1/2 c milk
- 1 large egg
- 2 tbsp butter, melted

RECIPE NOTES

You will need a silicone donut pan that you can cut down to fit inside your air fryer basket. Find the ones I use at AirFryerTools.com

INSTRUCTIONS

01 In a large bowl, whisk together flour, sugar, baking powder, baking soda, and salt.

02 In a separate bowl, whisk together sour cream, milk, eggs, and butter.

03 Add the wet ingredients to the dry and mix with a spoon or spatula until just combined. The batter will be lumpy. Don't overmix. Let batter rest while you prepare the pan and preheat air fryer.

04 Spray donut pan lightly with cooking oil to help prevent the donuts from sticking. Preheat air fryer at 350°F/176°C for a few minutes.

05 Spoon batter into each donut pan cavity until about 3/4 full. Bake in air fryer at 320°F/160°C for 7-9 minutes, until lightly golden brown.

06 Let cool in pan for about 5 minutes, then carefully remove.

07 Serve warm with your favorite pancake toppings!

Three Ingredient Bagels

Incredibly easy and fresh air fryer bagels ready in 10 minutes. Plus, you only need 3 ingredients. This dough also works great as a homemade pizza dough!

PREP TIME: 15 minutes **COOK TIME:** 7 minutes **TOTAL TIME:** 22 minutes **SERVES:** 3

RECIPE INGREDIENTS

BAGEL DOUGH

- ✅ 1 c flour
- ✅ 1 c Greek yogurt
- ✅ 2 tsp baking powder
- ✅ 1/4 tsp salt

EGG WASH

- ✅ 1 egg white
- ✅ 1 tsp water

RECIPE NOTES

Watch your bagels carefully in the air fryer as they burn easily.

While forming the bagels, have extra flour handy for your hands as it can be a little sticky.

Best served immediately.

INSTRUCTIONS

01. Mix dough ingredients together.

02. Form dough into 4 circles using your thumb to make a hole.

03. Beat egg with water and brush over tops.

04. Apply any topping you like, such as Everything Bagel seasoning, or enjoy as is.

05. Lightly spray the air fryer basket with cooking oil.

06. Cook at 300°F/150°C for 10 minutes flipping halfway until golden brown.

07. Remove from air fryer, allow to cool.

Buttery Sweet Monkey Bread

After making monkey bread in the air fryer, you'll never want to go back!
This monkey bread is delicate, buttery, and a long time family favorite!

PREP TIME: 10 minutes   **COOK TIME:** 20 minutes   **TOTAL TIME:** 30 minutes   **SERVES:** 6

RECIPE INGREDIENTS

BREAD

- 12 Rhodes White Dinner Rolls or any pre-made frozen dough, dough thawed to room temperature
- 1/2 c brown sugar
- 1 tsp cinnamon
- 4 tbsp butter melted

GLAZE

- 1/2 c powdered sugar
- 1-2 tbsp milk
- 1/2 tsp vanilla

TOOLS:

Use a 7" air fryer "cake barrel" or any oven safe dish. Find it at AirFryerTools.com.

INSTRUCTIONS

01. In a small bowl, mix together brown sugar and cinnamon.

02. In a separate bowl, melt a half stick of butter.

03. Use an oven safe pan that fits in your air fryer, lightly brush inside of pan with melted butter.

04. Once your rolls are thawed out to room temperature, cut them in half and roll each piece in butter, then dip into the sugar mixture, and place into pan. Repeat!

05. Once all your rolls are placed into the pan, pour any remaining butter and sugar on top.

06. Let rolls rise for 30 minutes in a preheated air fryer that is OFF, until rolls have risen, just to the top of the pan.

07. Carefully cover rolls with foil to prevent the top from burning. Be sure to tuck foil under to hold it in place. Bake at 340°F/170°C for 10-20 minutes. You will know bread is cooked when an instant read thermometer reads about 180°F/82°C.

08. While baking, make glaze by whisking powdered sugar, vanilla and milk until slightly runny.

09. Remove foil and bake for 1-3 more minutes to lightly brown the top. Carefully remove pan from air fryer (with oven mitts).

10. Let cool for just a few minutes and invert a plate over top of pan and turn the pan over onto plate.

11. Add glaze and enjoy.

Lemon Berry Baked Oatmeal

Enjoy this light, zesty, and fresh baked oatmeal in your air fryer! Topped with summer berries and Greek yogurt, you'll love this easy breakfast recipe.

PREP TIME: 15 minutes   **COOK TIME:** 12 minutes   **TOTAL TIME:** 27 minutes   **SERVES:** 2

RECIPE INGREDIENTS

- 1/2 c rolled oats
- 1/2 tsp baking powder
- 1/2 tsp ground cinnamon
- 1/4 tsp salt
- 1 tbsp brown sugar
- 1 lemon, you will use the zest and 1/2 of the juice from this lemon
- 1/2 c milk of your choice
- 1 egg
- 1 c berries of choice, 1/2 diced, 1/2 sliced; I did blueberries, strawberries, and blackberries
- 1/3 c slivered almonds
- 1/3 tsp nutmeg

TOOLS:

Use a 7" air fryer "cake barrel" or any oven safe dish. Find it at AirFryerTools.com.

INSTRUCTIONS

01 In a bowl, mix together the rolled oats, baking powder, cinnamon, salt, brown sugar, and zest from 1 lemon (you can use less zest if you don't want it to be as lemony).

02 In a separate bowl, mix together the milk, egg, and lemon juice from 1/2 of the zested lemon (you can add more or less lemon juice to your preference).

03 Combine and mix together the wet and dry ingredients and let it rest for 10 minutes.

04 While the oatmeal rests, prepare the berries. You can use any berries you want here, I did blueberries, strawberries, and blackberries. You want 1/2 cup diced berries and 1/2 cup sliced berries.

05 When the mixture is ready, spray an air fryer safe pan with non-stick spray oil.

06 Place the diced berries on the bottom, then pour the combined oatmeal mixture in.

07 Add the sliced berries on top. Then, sprinkle on almonds and nutmeg.

08 Cook in the air fryer at 300°F/150°C for 12 minutes. Check on the oatmeal after 10 minutes, if it's done then remove from the air fryer basket.

Optional Serving Suggestion: Enjoy with Greek yogurt on top!

Homemade Granola

Homemade Granola is healthy, tasty, and easy!
An air fryer recipe that everyone loves!

PREP TIME: 15 minutes   **COOK TIME:** 10 minutes   **TOTAL TIME:** 25 minutes   **SERVES:** 12

RECIPE INGREDIENTS

- 1 1/2 c old fashioned rolled oats
- 1/4 c unsweetened coconut flakes or shaved almonds
- 1/2 c shelled pumpkin seeds
- 2 tbsp flax seeds
- 2 tbsp honey (42 g)
- 2 tbsp real maple syrup (42 g)
- 2 tbsp coconut oil melted into liquid form, (substitute with butter or oil of choice)
- 1/4 tsp salt

INSTRUCTIONS

01. In a mixing bowl, combine rolled oats, coconut flakes, pumpkin seeds and flax seeds.

02. In a second bowl, add the coconut oil, honey, maple syrup, and salt. Stir to combine. They will combine easier if you heat them in the microwave for 15-30 seconds.

03. Drizzle the liquid mixture over the dry ingredients and gently toss/stir until evenly coated.

04. Place the granola in an even layer in the air fryer basket and cook for 4 minutes at 340°F/170°C.

05. Use a silicone spatula to separate and mix the granola mixture within the air fryer basket.

06. Cook for an additional 4 minutes and again stir the granola.

07. Cook for a further 2-3 minutes, or until the granola is a light golden brown.

08. Pour onto a parchment lined cookie sheet, spread evenly and let cool completely.

09. Enjoy with your favorite yogurt and berries.

10. Store in an airtight container.

Crunchy Breakfast Wrap

*For a speedy morning, use some leftover bacon and
fried eggs for a delicious breakfast crunch wrap!*

PREP TIME: 2 minutes   **COOK TIME:** 5 minutes   **TOTAL TIME:** 7 minutes   **SERVES:** 1

RECIPE INGREDIENTS

- ✓ 1 fried egg
- ✓ 1 flour tortilla, soft taco sized
- ✓ 1-2 slices of chopped bacon or sausage strips
- ✓ 1 tbsp Pico de gallo or salsa
- ✓ 2 tbsp shredded cheese

INSTRUCTIONS

01 Prepare the tortilla. Cut the radius of the tortilla, from the middle to one of the edges.

02 Place the fried or scrambled egg on a quarter of the tortilla next to the cut you just made. In the next quarter, place the sausage or bacon, and in the third quarter, place the pico or salsa. In the last quarter, place the cheese.

03 Fold the tortilla. Fold the tortilla by folding each quarter of the other, starting with the egg, until you have a triangle formed.

04 Cook in the air fryer. Lightly spray the air fryer basket and place the tortilla wrap inside. Lightly spray the top of the wrap and cook at 370°F/185°C for 5 minutes, or until the tortilla reaches desired crunchiness and the cheese is melted.

Toasted Breakfast Sandwich

PREP TIME: 20 minutes   **COOK TIME:** 6 minutes   **TOTAL TIME:** 26 minutes   **SERVES:** 1

RECIPE INGREDIENTS

- ✓ 2 slices soft white bread
- ✓ 2 slices of pre-cooked bacon or sausage strips
- ✓ 1 fried egg
- ✓ 1 slice of cheese

INSTRUCTIONS

01 Lightly spray the outside of each piece of bread, or lightly spray with oil of choice. Place a layer of fried eggs, breakfast sausage, and cheese on the first slice of bread, then cover with the second slice of bread to make a sandwich in the air fryer.

02 Air Fry at 360°F/182°C for 4 minutes, flip and cook for 2 more minutes.

NOTES

MAIN DISHES

NOTES

BEEF

Ground Beef in the Air Fryer

Cooking ground beef in your air fryer is healthier, quicker, and one of the easiest recipes around! Use it for soups, tacos, spaghetti sauce, enchiladas, and more!

PREP TIME: 5 minutes   **COOK TIME:** 8 minutes   **TOTAL TIME:** 13 minutes   **SERVES:** 4

RECIPE INGREDIENTS

- 1 lb ground beef, thawed if frozen
- seasonings to your taste

INSTRUCTIONS

01 Preheat air fryer to 400°F/200°C for 5 minutes.

02 Place beef in air fryer and break it up.

03 Cook in air fryer at 380°F/193°C for 4 minutes.

04 Stir beef and break apart larger pieces. Then cook at 380°F/193°C for another 3 minutes or until beef is evenly browned when stirred.

05 Season to taste and transfer to a bowl or large plate to cool completely.

06 Store in refrigerator for up to 4 days or freeze for up to 3 months.

Juicy Steak and Mushrooms Bites

These steak and mushroom bites can be prepped and ready in under 30 minutes.
You will be blown away by its tasty flavors and simplicity.

PREP TIME: 15 minutes   **COOK TIME:** 6 minutes   **TOTAL TIME:** 141 minutes   **SERVES:** 4

RECIPE INGREDIENTS

- ✔ 1 pound steak, cut into 1" cubes, pat dry (rib eye, tri-tip and New York strip)
- ✔ 8 oz mushrooms halved
- ✔ 1/2 onion sliced

MARINADE

- ✔ 1/2 c Worcestershire sauce (or teriyaki)
- ✔ 1/2 tbsp garlic powder
- ✔ salt and pepper to taste

INSTRUCTIONS

01. Prepare the steak, mushrooms, and onions. Combine them together in a bowl with the marinade ingredients. Mix until everything is well combined.

02. Cover, refrigerate and marinate for at least 2 hours.

03. Before cooking, preheat the air fryer at 400°F/200°C for 5 minutes.

04. Cook at 400°F/200°C for 6 minutes (or longer if your steak is cut larger and you want it cooked well done)!

05. Enjoy while hot.

RECIPE NOTES

If you prefer veggies cooked softer, you'll want to keep them seperate from the steak bites and cook them alone for 5-8 minutes, then add the steak bites. You can do this by splitting the marinade into two bowls.

38

Steak - Perfect Every Time

It is easy to get perfect results every time with your air fryer!
Top it off with delicious garlic herb butter. Yum!

PREP TIME: 20 minutes   **COOK TIME:** 13 minutes   **TOTAL TIME:** 33 minutes   **SERVES:** 4

RECIPE INGREDIENTS

- 2 Ribeye steaks each 1 1/2 inches thick
- avocado oil
- salt and pepper

GARLIC HERB BUTTER

- 2 tbsp unsalted butter softened
- 1/2 tbsp chopped fresh parsley
- 1/2 tsp minced garlic
- 1/4 tsp Worcestershire sauce
- 1/3 tsp salt

RECIPE NOTES

Steak will continue to cook while resting. Consider pulling steak from air fryer when it's 3 degrees away from reaching desired internal temperature. See index for recommended temperatures in F and C.

INSTRUCTIONS

01 Temper the steak by letting it sit at room temperature for 20-30 minutes.

02 Prepare the garlic butter by mixing together the softened butter, parsley, garlic, Worcestershire, and salt. Set aside.

03 Pat steaks dry with paper towels, then rub a little bit of oil over the steak and bottom of air fryer basket. Liberally season steaks with salt and pepper.

04 Preheat air fryer to 400°F/200°C for 10 minutes.

05 Once preheated, immediately place steaks in air fryer.

06 Cook for 6-12 minutes, flipping and rotating halfway through. Cooking time will vary depending on your air fryer and thickness of steaks. Internal temperature of steak should be 130°F - 135°F for medium-rare or 140°F - 145°F for medium.

07 Top with garlic butter and allow to rest for 1/2 the time it took to cook.

Meatballs with Barbecue Glaze (Freezer Friendly)

These easy homemade meatballs with a sweet glaze recipe are tasty and simple. Prepare and freeze these meatballs and then cook them later in the air fryer or your oven!

RECIPE INGREDIENTS

MEATBALLS

- ✓ 1 lb ground beef
- ✓ 4 oz evaporated milk
- ✓ 1/3 c oatmeal
- ✓ 1/3 c saltine cracker crumbs
- ✓ 1 large egg
- ✓ 1/4 c chopped onion
- ✓ 1/4 tsp garlic powder
- ✓ 1 tsp salt
- ✓ 1/4 tsp pepper
- ✓ 3/4 tsp chili powder

GLAZE

- ✓ 1 c ketchup
- ✓ 1/2 c brown sugar
- ✓ 1/4 tsp liquid smoke*
- ✓ 1/4 tsp garlic powder
- ✓ 2 tbsp chopped onion

RECIPE NOTES

- Serve on top of pasta tossed in olive oil and parmesan cheese, rice, or mashed potatoes.
- *If you don't have liquid smoke, you can substitute it with 1/2 tsp of Worcestershire sauce and 1 tsp of malt vinegar.
- If you want to add more punch to your meatballs, add 1/2 tsp of Tony's spice to the meatball mixture.

INSTRUCTIONS

01 Mix all the meatball ingredients together in a bowl.

02 Using a cookie scoop or spoon, form the mixture into meatballs. You can make the meatballs whatever size you want, however I recommend about 1-2 tbsp of mixture for each meatball.

03 To freeze the meatballs, place on a cookie sheet lined with parchment paper. Cover the meatballs with plastic wrap and place the cookie sheet in the freezer for 1-2 hours or until very firm.

04 Once frozen, remove the meatballs from the freezer and store them in a resealable plastic bag or air-tight container.

GLAZE

01 Mix all the glaze ingredients together on the stovetop over low/medium heat until the sugar is dissolved.

02 Let the glaze cool and then place the glaze in a container in the freezer. It will freeze soft and be easily scooped out later. You can also make the glaze the day you are serving the meatballs.

TO COOK IN AIR FRYER

01 Once you are ready to cook your frozen meatballs, remove the number of meatballs you need from the freezer and preheat the air fryer at 400°F/200°C for 5 minutes.

02 Spray the air fryer basket with oil then layer the meatballs inside.

03 Cook for 15 minutes at 350°F/176°C. At the halfway point, stir the meatballs.

04 During the last 2 minutes, spoon some of the glaze over the meatballs. You will want to save some of the glaze for serving your meatballs.

05 Once the meatballs register an internal temperature of 165°F/74°C, they are ready!

Steak Fajitas

*This is a super easy dinner that can be made ahead of time or
even as a freezer meal! It's also a major crowd pleaser!*

PREP TIME: 8 hours 15 mins   **COOK TIME:** 14 mins   **TOTAL TIME:** 8 hours 30 mins   **SERVES:** 6

RECIPE INGREDIENTS

- ✓ 1 1/2 lbs boneless skinless top sirloin steak (or other steak), cut into strips crosswise
- ✓ 1-2 peppers, sliced
- ✓ 1/2-1 onion, sliced
- ✓ 2 tbsp lime juice
- ✓ 2 tbsp soy sauce
- ✓ 2 tbsp oil
- ✓ 1/2 tsp ground cumin
- ✓ 1/2 tsp chili powder
- ✓ 1/2 tsp dried oregano
- ✓ 1/4 tsp black pepper
- ✓ 2 tsp minced garlic (about 6 cloves)

INSTRUCTIONS

01. Combine marinade ingredients, then pour marinade over steak and veggies in a re-sealable plastic bag or a bowl. Seal or cover and let it rest no longer than 24 hours.

02. Preheat the air fryer at 400°F/200°C for 5 minutes.

03. Place the steak and veggies in the air fryer basket and cook for 14 minutes at 360°F/182°C, stirring at the halfway point.

Honey Garlic Meatballs

These honey garlic meatballs are always a hit!
Serve over rice or enjoy as a standalone appetizer.

PREP TIME: 5 minutes   **COOK TIME:** 10 minutes   **TOTAL TIME:** 15 minutes   **SERVES:** 8

RECIPE INGREDIENTS

- 1/4 c brown sugar
- 1/3 c honey (111 grams)
- 1/2 c ketchup (136 grams)
- 2 tbsp low sodium soy sauce (30 ml)
- 3 cloves garlic minced (or 1 1/2 tsp)
- 1 lb 12 oz frozen fully cooked meatballs

INSTRUCTIONS

01   In a medium bowl, whisk together the brown sugar, honey, ketchup, soy sauce, and garlic.

02   Place frozen meatballs in air fryer in a single layer and cook at 350°F/176°C for 8 minutes. Then pour glaze over the top and cook for 2 minutes longer.

44

Tasty Meatloaf with Tangy Glaze

Even my pickiest eaters who don't care for meatloaf LOVE this recipe!
And making it in an air fryer saves so much time too!

PREP TIME: 20 minutes   **COOK TIME:** 25 minutes   **TOTAL TIME:** 45 minutes   **SERVES:** 6

RECIPE INGREDIENTS

- 1 c crushed saltines, about 30 crackers
- 1 c milk
- 1/4 c fresh parsley, minced
- 2 large eggs lightly beaten
- 2 tsp onion powder
- 3 garlic cloves finely minced or 1 tsp garlic powder
- 1 tbsp Dijon mustard
- 3 tbsp Worcestershire sauce
- 1 1/2 tsp coarse Kosher salt
- 1/2 tsp coarse black pepper
- 2 pounds ground meat (I use half ground beef/half ground pork)

GLAZE (COMBINE)

- 1 c ketchup or BBQ sauce, or a combination
- 3 tbsp brown sugar
- 3 tbsp red wine vinegar

INSTRUCTIONS

01. Preheat your air fryer at 380°F/193°C for 5 minutes.

02. Mix the crushed saltines and milk together and let it sit for about 10 minutes.

03. Add in the rest of the ingredients besides the meat and mix it together really well. Then fold in the meat. Do not overmix.

FORM THE MEATLOAF (TWO OPTIONS)

01. Option 1. Shape the meat mixture into even palm sized patties or loaves. The trick with cooking meat in the air fryer is that it needs to be the same thickness throughout the entire patty so it can cook evenly. Set it on parchment paper for ease of cleaning.

02. Option 2. Use a silicone mold dish to make meatloaf bites. Fill each of the molds with about 4 tbsp of the meatloaf mixture.

AIR FRY

01. Cook the meatloaf in the air fryer for 15 minutes at 380°F/193°C. Then glaze the meatloaf with half of the glaze sauce. (Cooking time will be relatively the same for either method).

02. Cook for another 6-10 minutes or until the meat thermometer registers at 160°F/71°C with an instant read food thermometer.

Quick and Easy Stuffed Peppers

Tasty and quick stuffed peppers in the air fryer are the perfect weekday meal!
And they can be prepared ahead and frozen.

PREP TIME: 20 minutes   **COOK TIME:** 15 minutes   **TOTAL TIME:** 35 minutes   **SERVES:** 6

RECIPE INGREDIENTS

- 6 bell peppers, any color
- 1 lb ground beef
- 1 packet taco seasoning (about 1 to 2 tbsp)
- 1 c cooked rice
- 3 green onions chopped
- 1/2 c black beans
- 1 c frozen corn, thawed
- 1 c shredded cheese optional, plus more for topping
- toppings such as salsa, sour cream and/or tortilla chips (optional)

INSTRUCTIONS

01. Brown the ground beef and drain, if needed. Add the taco seasoning as instructed by the package.

02. Add the rice, onions, beans, corn, and cheese (if using) and stir it all together.

03. Slice the tops off the peppers and clean out the inside, cut the peppers in half lengthwise, then stuff them with the ground beef mixture.

04. Place up to 6 peppers in the air fryer basket and cook for 10 minutes at 350°F/176°C.

05. Sprinkle remaining cheese on top of the peppers and cook for an additional 5 minutes or until the cheese melts and the peppers are tender.

06. Serve plain or topped with salsa and sour cream.

MAKE AHEAD INSTRUCTIONS

01. Prepare the stuffed peppers as written. Instead of cooking them immediately, individually wrap them in plastic wrap. Place the peppers on a cookie sheet, then place in the freezer. Once frozen, store in a plastic bag.

02. Pull out the peppers the morning you plan on using them and place in the refrigerator. Then, cook at 350°F/176°C for 10 minutes. Check on them, top with cheese, then cook for an additional 5 minutes. Check internal temperature to be sure they are heated through.

Delicious Zucchini Boats

A quick and easy, low carb dinner in the air fryer! These air fryer zucchini boats are simple to make and are bursting with all the right, fresh summer flavors.

PREP TIME: 15 minutes   **COOK TIME:** 10 minutes   **TOTAL TIME:** 25 minutes   **SERVES:** 4

RECIPE INGREDIENTS

- 1 pound ground beef or ground turkey
- 1/2 onion diced
- 1/2 tsp Italian seasoning
- salt and pepper to taste
- 12 oz marinara sauce
- 2 medium zucchini
- parmesan cheese or other favorite cheese

INSTRUCTIONS

01 Make the marinara meat sauce that will go inside the zucchini boats by browning the ground beef. Add the onion, Italian seasoning, salt, pepper, and marinara sauce.

02 Take the zucchini, cut in half lengthwise and scoop out the seeds. Pat the inside dry with a paper towel. Lightly mist with oil and sprinkle with salt.

03 Place the zucchini in the air fryer basket and cook at 380°F/193°C for 8-10 minutes until cooked through. The cooking time will depend greatly on the size of your zucchini and how cooked through you want it to be. Check on the zucchini after 5 minutes and adjust as needed. Once your zucchini reaches its desired tenderness, pat dry any excess moisture from the zucchini, add the marinara meat sauce, sprinkle on parmesan cheese, and cook for an additional 2-3 minutes, or until cheese is melted.

04 Carefully remove from the air fryer basket and enjoy!

Easy Asian Beef and Veggies

Fully-flavored and quick-to-assemble, you are going to love this simple Asian beef and veggies dish.

PREP TIME: 70 minutes **COOK TIME:** 14 minutes **TOTAL TIME:** 84 minutes **SERVES:** 4

RECIPE INGREDIENTS

- 1 lb sirloin steak cut into strips
- 1/2 onion sliced
- 1 medium red pepper sliced
- 1 c sugar snap peas
- 2-3 c cooked hot rice
- 3 sliced scallions
- 2 tsp sesame seeds

MARINADE

- 6 cloves garlic, minced
- 4 tbsp fresh ginger, grated
- 1/2 tsp red chili flakes
- 1 c soy sauce
- 1/2 c rice vinegar
- 2 tsp sesame oil
- 2/3 c brown sugar
- 1/2 c water
- **Optional:** 2 tsp Chinese 5 spice powder

INSTRUCTIONS

01. Prepare the steak, onion, red pepper, and snap peas. The steak should be sliced against the muscle length.

02. In a bowl, mix the marinade ingredients together. Set aside half for the glaze.

03. Add the beef and veggies to a medium sized bowl or a resealable bag, add the marinade and toss or massage to coat the steak and veggies. Marinate for at least 1 hour.

04. Preheat the air fryer at 400°F/200°C for 5 minutes.

05. Spray the air fryer basket with avocado oil.

06. Transfer the veggies to the air fryer basket and cook at 400°F/200°C for 8 minutes.

07. Remove the steak strips from the marinade. Discard the marinade. Add the steak to the veggies in the air fryer basket and cook for an additional 4-6 minutes, or until the internal temperature of the steak is 135-145°F/57.2-62.7°C.

08. Remove from the air fryer basket and serve over cooked rice garnished with sliced scallion, sesame seeds, and glaze, if desired.

GLAZE INSTRUCTIONS

01. Use your reserved marinade (half of the marinade ingredients – make sure you are **not** using the leftover marinade from marinating the steak and veggies) to make a glaze or sauce.

02. Heat the reserved marinade in a saucepan until simmering.

03. Mix together 1 tablespoon cornstarch with 1 tablespoon of cold water until it is a smooth paste.

04. Add the cornstarch mixture to the simmering marinade and whisk until it thickens and reaches desired consistency.

05. If you want to make the sauce thicker, combine equal parts of cornstarch and cold water together and add it to the simmering sauce. Typically, 1 tablespoon of cornstarch thickens 1 cup of liquid.

FREEZER MEAL INSTRUCTIONS

01. If you want to freeze this meal for later use, make only half of the written marinade ingredients. When you are ready to enjoy this recipe, make another half of the marinade for a glaze or sauce.

02. First, combine the beef, veggies, and the marinade together in a resealable plastic bag. Then, date and place the bag flat in the freezer.

03. Take out of the freezer the morning or night before using. Since the marinade is a soy sauce base, sometimes it can overwhelm the beef and veggies. To avoid this, about 3 hours before cooking, place a strainer over a large bowl, dump the contents into the strainer. Cover with the plate and place back in the refrigerator until you are ready to cook.

04. Preheat the air fryer at 400°F/200°C for 5 minutes. Place the meat and veggies into the air fryer basket and discard the marinade. Cook for 8 minutes at 400°F/200°C, checking on it at the halfway point.

05. Make a glaze with half of the marinade ingredients, if desired. See "Glaze Instructions".

06. Remove from the air fryer and enjoy with rice, sliced scallion, sesame seeds, and glaze, if desired.

Juicy Roast Beef and Tender Vegetables

Fall in love with this juicy and tender roast beef in the air fryer, cooked at the same time as the veggies!

PREP TIME: 40 minutes   **COOK TIME:** 42 minutes   **TOTAL TIME:** 82 minutes   **SERVES:** 4

RECIPE INGREDIENTS

- 3 pound roast or smaller *see note*
- 1 1/2 pounds Yukon gold potatoes
- 1 yellow onion cut into eighths
- 12 oz baby carrots or 3 whole carrots
- oil of your choice
- salt and pepper to taste
- 2 sprigs fresh rosemary
- fresh thyme, to taste

RECIPE NOTES

I recommend a quality-cut 2 pound beef roast, like tri-tip or sirloin with dark red coloring. The traditional chuck or shoulder roast meat requires more of a slow cook to get tender. In an air fryer, they will come out tough.

INSTRUCTIONS

01. Pat meat dry, trim excess fat and let stand at room temperature for 30 minutes.

02. While the meat tempers, prep your spices/ seasoning. I used fresh rosemary and thyme. You can use dry spices or any other spices of your choice.

03. Once the meat has tempered rub a little bit of oil all over your meat. You don't need a lot here, just enough to lightly cover the outside. The oil will help the outside brown and the spices adhere to the meat.

04. Liberally salt the meat and rub it in. Do a little more than you think is necessary.

05. Season the meat with spices and pepper rubbing it in well.

06. Preheat air fryer at 400°F/200°C for 5 minutes.

07. Place meat in air fryer basket. Tuck any smaller ends of the roast into itself so that it cooks evenly. Cook at 400°F/200°C for 10-12 minutes.

08. While the meat cooks, prepare the vegetables.

09. For the potatoes: wash, dry, and cut into equal sized cubes. About 1 inch thick, but you can make them as big or as small as you want. Either directly spray with oil and salt on your cutting board or toss in a bowl with oil and salt.

10. For the carrots: If using whole carrots, cut into equal bite-sized pieces. Wash, and pat dry.

11. For the onions: cut into eighths through the root end. Combine with carrots and spray with oil, then salt, and mix together.

12. Flip the roast, then cover with the potatoes, onions, and carrots. Cook for 20 minutes at 360°F/182°C.

13. After 10 minutes, check on the roast with an instant read food thermometer. If the roast internal temperature is 145F it is cooked to Medium. Take the roast out of air fryer basket and transfer to a plate and tent with foil. Stir the vegetables and finish cooking for the last 10 minutes.

14. If your meat hasn't registered at 145°F/63°C, stir the vegetables, flip the roast and cook for the remaining 10 minutes. Check the meat again and if needed continue to cook for an additional 5 minutes at 360°F/182°C.

15. Repeat last step until roast reaches 145°F/63°C. Check the temperature guide if you prefer your meat cooked to a different level.

16. Once roast is cooked through, tent the roast in foil for 10 minutes.

Homemade Hamburger Patties

Add a little pizzazz to your burgers with some extra seasoning!
These cook up so fast in the air fryer and clean up is simple!

PREP TIME: 15 minutes   **COOK TIME:** 8 minutes   **TOTAL TIME:** 23 minutes   **SERVES:** 4

RECIPE INGREDIENTS

- 1 lb ground beef
- 1 tbsp worcestershire sauce
- 1/2 tsp garlic powder
- 1 tsp salt
- 1 tsp pepper
- pinch cayenne pepper

RECIPE NOTES

Once patties are cooked through, place a slice of your favorite cheese on top of each patty, and close the air fryer door and DON'T turn it back on, the cheese will melt perfectly in a minute or two.

INSTRUCTIONS

01 Combine all the ingredients together in a bowl.

02 Form 3-4 patties.

03 Preheat the air fryer at 400°F/200°C for 5 minutes.

04 Place the patties in the air fryer basket and cook at 380°F/193°C for 4-8 minutes. The cooking time will vary depending on the thickness of the patties. It will be finished when the internal temperature of the patties reaches 160°F/71°C.

Effortless Hamburgers in Minutes!

Simple air fryer hamburgers are juicy, easy, and a kid-approved meal!
Using frozen patties makes them very convenient.

PREP TIME: 2 minutes   **COOK TIME:** 17 minutes   **TOTAL TIME:** 19 minutes   **SERVES:** 4

RECIPE INGREDIENTS

- ✅ 4 frozen hamburger patties
- ✅ **Optional:** sliced onions, cheese

RECIPE NOTES

To toast hamburger buns: after wiping the inside of the basket, place buns, open side up, in basket and cook at 400°F/200°C for 2-3 minutes

INSTRUCTIONS

01. Place frozen patties in the air fryer basket, do not overlap patties.

02. Cook at 370°F/187°C for 7-10 minutes.

03. Flip burgers and cook for 6-7 more minutes at 370°F/187°C or until done.

04. Optional Sautéed Onions: Add sliced onions during the second round of cooking (the last 6-7 minutes). Lightly spray the onions and sprinkle them with salt. Spread them on the burgers and in the basket.

05. To add cheese, place cheese over fully cooked hamburger patty and close air fryer for 1-2 minutes (leave it off) and the cheese will magically melt!

Taco Foldover Quesadilla

You'll love this crunchy twist on the traditional taco night!

PREP TIME: 20 minutes   **COOK TIME:** 5 minutes   **TOTAL TIME:** 25 minutes   **SERVES:** 4

RECIPE INGREDIENTS

- 1/2 lb ground beef
- 2 tsp taco seasoning
- 4 regular soft taco sized flour tortillas
- 4 tbsp sour cream
- 1/2 c shredded cheese
- 1/2 c Pico de gallo

INSTRUCTIONS

01. Brown ground beef. Season with taco seasoning, stir, then drain and set aside.

02. Lay tortilla flat, fold in half, open back up, then fold in half opposite direction, and open up again. The fold marks create a center point and 4 equal quadrants. Cut along one line going from the center of the tortilla to the right edge. Top right quadrant is for the sour cream (spread evenly), bottom right - single layer of ground beef, bottom left - single layer of shredded cheese, top left - single layer of pico de gallo. (The cut is between the sour cream and ground beef.)

03. Take the top right sour cream section and fold it over onto the top left pico de gallo section. Then continue by folding that section down onto the bottom left cheese section and again onto the bottom right, until it is a multi-layer triangle.

04. Place folded quesadillas into air fryer basket that is lightly sprayed with avocado oil. Then lightly mist the top of the tortilla.

05. Air fry at 380°F/193°C for 4-5 minutes, until golden brown and crisp on the outside, rotating if needed.

Fast Beef Enchiladas

Want to make tasty enchiladas in minutes? You have got to try this easy and simple air fryer enchilada recipe! Use these homemade options, or to save even more time, buy store bought enchilada sauce and seasoning!

PREP TIME: 30 minutes   **COOK TIME:** 4 minutes   **TOTAL TIME:** 34 minutes   **SERVES:** 8

RECIPE INGREDIENTS

SPICE MIX
(MAKES 1 OZ OF MIX)

- 1 tsp onion powder
- 1 tsp garlic powder
- 1 tbsp cumin powder
- 1 tbsp paprika
- 1 tbsp dried oregano
- 1/2 -1 tsp cayenne pepper optional, spiciness

ENCHILADA SAUCE

- 2 tbsp olive oil
- 3 tbsp flour
- 2 c chicken stock or broth
- 8 oz can of tomato sauce
- 1/4 tsp salt
- 1/4 tsp pepper

BEEF

- 1 tbsp olive oil
- 2 cloves garlic minced
- 1 onion finely chopped (about 1 c)
- 1 lb ground beef
- 14 oz can refried beans
- 14 oz can black beans drained

INSTRUCTIONS

01. If making homemade spice mix, combine ingredients and set aside (or use your favorite taco seasoning).

02. For the homemade enchilada sauce, heat oil in a large saucepan over medium heat and add flour. Mix to combine into a paste, then cook for about 1 minute, stirring constantly.

03. Whisk in 1/2 cup chicken broth until it thickens to a smooth paste.

04. Add remaining chicken broth, tomato sauce, salt, pepper and 2 tbsp of the spice mix (or your favorite taco seasoning).

05. Increase heat to medium high. Cook for 3 to 5 minutes, whisking regularly, until the sauce comes to a boil and thickens to the consistency of thick syrup. Remove from heat.

06. Next, cook garlic and onion in a tablespoon of oil for 2 minutes.

07. Add ground beef and cook, breaking it up as you go. Add remaining spice mix during the last few minutes of cooking. Drain meat, if desired.

08. Add refried beans, black beans, about 1/4-1/2 cup of Enchilada Sauce, salt, and pepper. Mix and cook for 2 minutes then remove from the stove.

09. Make a foil sling that fits your air fryer basket, leaving room for air flow.

ENCHILADAS

- 8-12 tortillas – this will depend on the size of tortillas you use, I used medium sized and was able to get 12 enchiladas

- 1 1/2 c grated melting cheese Fiesta blend, Monterey Jack, cheddar cheese, you can choose any cheese you love!

- Cilantro for garnish

- 1/4 - 1/2 c enchilada sauce

10. Place desired amount of beef mixture inside tortilla. Roll up then place in the air fryer basket, seam side down. Repeat. The amount of enchiladas that you will be able to put in your air fryer basket will depend on its size. You may have to cook in batches, or freeze some for later!

11. Pour sauce over the enchiladas, top with cheese, bake for 4 minutes at 350°F/176°C, or until the cheese is melted.

12. Carefully remove from the air fryer basket and enjoy as is or with your favorite enchilada toppings!

Cheeseburger Egg Rolls

Whip up these tasty cheeseburger egg rolls, inspired by the delicious ones from the Cheesecake Factory! And you can do it in less than 30 minutes in your air fryer!

PREP TIME: 15 minutes   **COOK TIME:** 8 minutes   **TOTAL TIME:** 23 minutes   **SERVES:** 6 people

RECIPE INGREDIENTS

- 1 lb lean ground beef
- 1/4 c minced onions
- 1/4 c pickle relish
- 1 tbsp Worcestershire sauce
- 6 slices American cheese
- 1 package egg roll wrappers or spring roll wrappers
- egg wash

DIPPING SAUCE

- 1/2 c mayonnaise
- 2 tbsp ketchup
- 2 tbsp pickle relish
- 1-2 splashes red wine vinegar
- 1 pinch garlic powder
- 1 pinch onion powder

INSTRUCTIONS

01. Brown 1 pound of ground beef, drain excess grease, then add onions, pickle relish, and Worcestershire sauce, blend. Stir in cheese until melted/blended. Set aside and let it cool slightly.

02. Scoop approximately a third of a cup of the mixture onto center of the spring roll wrapper and spread out to form a small rectangle that stops about an inch and a half away from the left and right edges.

03. Using a brush, apply the egg wash across the top of wrapper. Fold over the left and right sides of the wrapper and then roll from the bottom towards the top, allowing the egg wash to seal the roll.

04. Place seam-side down in the air fryer basket. Lightly spray with oil and cook at 380°F/193°C for 5-8 minutes or until lightly browned, flipping half way through cooking.

05. While the wrappers are cooking in the air fryer, mix together the dipping sauce ingredients until well combined.

Easy Taco Bites

You don't have to be eating keto or low carb to enjoy these mini taco bites. My whole family loves them and they are ready in 30 minutes or less (and they freeze well too)!

PREP TIME: 10 minutes   **COOK TIME:** 15 minutes   **TOTAL TIME:** 25 minutes   **SERVES:** 6

RECIPE INGREDIENTS

- 1 lb ground beef
- 3 tbsp taco seasoning
- 8 large eggs
- 1 1/2 c Mexican blend shredded cheese, divided

INSTRUCTIONS

01. Cook the ground beef in the air fryer. Crumble and spread apart beef in the air fryer basket. Cook at 380°F/193°C for 4 minutes. Stir the beef with a silicone spatula. Add taco seasoning and cook at 350°F/175°C for 3 minutes.

02. Whisk together the eggs in a medium bowl. Add in about 1 cup cheese and ground beef. Stir together

03. Place 9-10 silicone muffin liners in the air fryer basket. Add 1/4 cup of mixture to the liners.

04. Cook at 330°F/165°C for 10 minutes. Top with cheese. Cook for an additional 3 minutes.

05. Let the taco bites rest for several minutes and enjoy.

NOTES

POULTRY

How to Make Juicy Chicken Breasts

If you're not careful, it's easy to dry out chicken in the air fryer!
Follow these tips for all of your chicken recipes for excellent results every time.
Use chicken as a main dish or to complement your favorite salad or pasta bowl!

PREP TIME: 5 minutes   **COOK TIME:** 10 minutes   **TOTAL TIME:** 15 minutes   **SERVES:** 4

RECIPE INGREDIENTS

- 4 boneless skinless chicken breasts, about 6 oz each
- 1 tsp salt
- 3/4 tsp garlic powder
- 3/4 tsp onion powder
- 1/2 tsp dried parsley
- 1/2 tsp smoked paprika
- pinch cayenne pepper
- olive or avocado oil spray

RECIPE NOTES

Use an instant read meat thermometer to ensure your chicken doesn't overcook and dry out. Find my favorite at AirFryerTools.com.

INSTRUCTIONS

01. Pound the thicker end of each chicken breast to even it out so they will cook more evenly. Pat chicken dry with paper towel.

02. In a small bowl, combine salt, garlic powder, onion powder, parsley, paprika, and cayenne pepper.

03. Spritz chicken with oil and rub to coat. Season both sides of chicken with the seasoning.

04. Place chicken in the air fryer basket in a single layer, no overlapping.

05. Cook at 380°F/193°C for about 10-15 minutes, turning halfway, until cooked through and instant read thermometer inserted into center of thickest part reads about 160°F.

06. Time will vary depending on the thickness of your chicken and the wattage of your air fryer.

07. Chicken is done when the internal temperature reaches 165ºF/74ºC. However, when you remove chicken from heat, it continues to cook for a few minutes more (referred to as carryover cooking).

08. If you let the chicken rest for 5-10 minutes, it will finish cooking to 165ºF/74ºC and the juices will redistribute and you'll have amazing results, no matter how you season it!

How to Air Fry Frozen Chicken

Can you cook frozen chicken in the air fryer? The answer is YES!
Note that the larger your chicken, the longer it will take to cook through.
Make sure you have an instant read thermometer!

PREP TIME: 10 minutes   **COOK TIME:** 23 minutes   **TOTAL TIME:** 33 minutes   **SERVES:** 4

RECIPE INGREDIENTS

- ✅ 5-8 frozen chicken tenderloins or 1-2 frozen chicken breasts
- ✅ avocado oil

HOMEMADE BBQ RUB (OR USE YOUR FAVORITE BRAND OF RUB)

- ✅ 1/4 c chili powder
- ✅ 1 tbsp paprika
- ✅ 1 tbsp thyme
- ✅ 2 tsp salt
- ✅ 2 tsp garlic powder
- ✅ 1 tsp black pepper
- ✅ 1 tsp ground cumin
- ✅ 1 tsp cayenne pepper
- ✅ 1 tbsp brown sugar

INSTRUCTIONS

01. Rinse chicken with tepid water to remove any ice and pat dry.

02. Lightly spray the chicken with avocado oil. Then season to taste. If you have leftover BBQ seasoning, save it in a container for later use.

03. Place the chicken in the air fryer basket, evenly spaced. Cook at 360°F/182°C for 15 minutes. Tenders are usually done in 15 minutes. For chicken breasts, flip the chicken and cook for an additional 8-12 minutes, or until the internal temp reads 160-162°F/71-72°C.

04. Tent the chicken for a couple of minutes to allow juices to redistribute and finish cooking to 165°F/74°C.

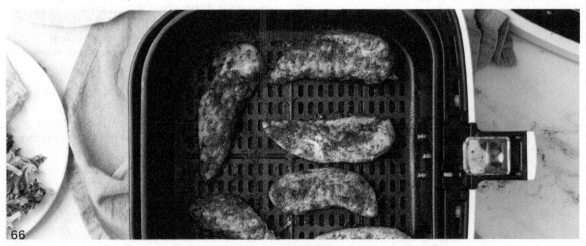

Fast Juicy Chicken Thighs

Amazing taste from these chicken thighs that are seasoned just right and cooked to perfection. Enjoy this chicken as is or use them for street tacos, salads, or pasta!

PREP TIME: 5 minutes   **COOK TIME:** 12 minutes   **TOTAL TIME:** 17 minutes   **SERVES:** 8

RECIPE INGREDIENTS

- ✅ 2 lbs boneless skinless chicken thighs
- ✅ 2 tsp avocado oil or other oil
- ✅ 2 tsp chili powder
- ✅ 1 tsp ground cumin
- ✅ 1 tsp garlic powder
- ✅ 1 tsp salt
- ✅ 1/2 tsp pepper
- ✅ pinch cayenne pepper

RECIPE NOTES

If desired, warm tortilla shells in the air fryer for 2 minutes at 350°F/176°C. Place a small air fryer rack over the top to keep them from blowing up into the heating element.

INSTRUCTIONS

01 In a small bowl, combine chili powder, cumin, garlic powder, salt, pepper, and cayenne pepper.

02 Pat chicken dry with paper towels, rub with oil, and sprinkle evenly on both sides with spice mixture.

03 Place chicken in air fryer basket and cook at 400°F/200°C for 12-16 minutes, or until chicken registers 175°F/80°C. Flip halfway through cooking, if desired.

04 Let chicken cool slightly, then shred or chop into bite-size pieces. Divide between taco shells and top with favorite toppings. Serve with lime wedges. Chicken may also be served over salad.

Savory Whole Chicken

This Whole Chicken is one of the easiest air fryer recipes. All you need is an hour to make this amazing, tender chicken. And it tastes better than what you'll find in a store!

PREP TIME: 5 minutes   **COOK TIME:** 60 minutes   **TOTAL TIME:** 65 minutes   **SERVES:** 4

RECIPE INGREDIENTS

- 4- 4 1/2 lb chicken
- 1 1/2 tsp avocado oil
- 1 tsp rosemary
- 1 tsp oregano
- 1 tsp pepper
- 1/2 tsp thyme
- 1/2 tsp sage
- 1/2 tsp ground mustard
- 1/2 tsp garlic powder
- 1/2 tsp onion powder
- 1/4 tsp basil
- 1 1/2 tsp kosher salt

INSTRUCTIONS

01 Preheat the air fryer at 400°F/200°C for 5 minutes.

02 Combine all the seasonings in a small bowl.

03 Rinse and pat chicken dry and massage oil then seasoning mix all over the chicken.

04 Place the chicken in air fryer basket, breast side down, cook at 350°F/176°C for 40 minutes.

05 Flip the chicken breast side up and cook at 350°F/176°C for an additional 25 minutes. During last 10 minutes, check internal temperature, cooking in 3-5 minute intervals until chicken reaches 165°F/74°C. Take basket out of air fryer and let chicken rest for about 10 minutes before carving.

RECIPE NOTES

A 4- 4 1/2 lb chicken fits easily in a air fryer basket that is 9"x9" and about 4" deep.

Quick & Easy Turkey Breast

*You'll be amazed at how juicy and tender a
turkey breast is when roasted in the air fryer!*

PREP TIME: 10 minutes   **COOK TIME:** 60 minutes   **TOTAL TIME:** 70 minutes   **SERVES:** 5

RECIPE INGREDIENTS

- 4 lb turkey breast
- 1 tbsp olive oil
- 2 tsp kosher salt optional

SEASONING

- 1/2 tbsp kosher salt
- 1/2 tbsp brown sugar
- 1/2 tsp paprika
- 1/2 tsp black pepper
- 3/4 tsp dried thyme
- 3/4 tsp dried rosemary
- 1/2 tsp dried sage
- 1/4 tsp garlic powder
- 1/4 tsp onion powder

INSTRUCTIONS

01. Rub 1/2 tbsp of oil all over the turkey breast. Season both sides with salt and turkey seasoning then rub in the remaining half tbsp of oil over the skin side.

02. Preheat the air fryer at 350°F/176°C and cook skin side down 20 minutes, turn over and cook about 30 to 40 minutes more or until the internal temperature is 155-160°F/68-71°C using an instant-read thermometer. The cooking time will depend on the size of your breast.

03. Let it rest 10 minutes to allow the turkey to finish cooking and the juices to redistribute before carving.

Rosemary Ranch Chicken

Tasty and simple air fryer rosemary chicken is one for the books!
Packed with flavor, this one will be a fast family favorite!

PREP TIME: 10 minutes   **COOK TIME:** 15 minutes   **TOTAL TIME:** 25 minutes   **SERVES:** 4

RECIPE INGREDIENTS

- 1/2 c ranch salad dressing
- 1/4 c worcestershire sauce
- 2 tbsp fresh lemon juice or red wine vinegar
- 1 tbsp finely chopped fresh rosemary
- 1 tsp salt
- 1/4 tsp black pepper
- 1 1/2 - 2 lb boneless chicken breasts, about 2-4 chicken breasts

RECIPE NOTES

Cooking time may vary depending on air fryer and chicken breast size. Use a meat thermometer to ensure your chicken doesn't overcook and dry out.

INSTRUCTIONS

01 For the marinade, whisk together all the ingredients until well-combined.

02 Pound the thicker side of chicken breast until it matches the thinner side, which will help chicken cook evenly. Alternatively, you could carefully butterfly chicken.

03 Place chicken in shallow dish or re-sealable plastic bag and pour the marinade over the chicken, turning the chicken to coat evenly. Cover the dish and refrigerate for 8-12 hours.

04 Place chicken in the air fryer basket in a single layer, no overlapping. You may have to cook in batches.

05 Cook at 380°F/193°C for about 10-15 minutes, turning halfway, until cooked through and instant read thermometer inserted into center of thickest part reads 160°F/71°C. Total time will depend on the thickness of your chicken. Let the chicken rest in the basket for about 5 minutes to finish cooking and redistribute juices.

Easy Honey Balsamic Chicken

With a simple spice rub and honey balsamic sauce,
there's lots of flavor and deliciousness to enjoy!

PREP TIME: 40 minutes   **COOK TIME:** 10 minutes   **TOTAL TIME:** 50 minutes   **SERVES:** 4

RECIPE INGREDIENTS

CHICKEN

- 2 pounds boneless skinless chicken breast
- 1 tsp olive oil
- 1/2 tsp kosher salt
- 1/4 tsp black pepper
- 1/2 tsp paprika
- 3/4 tsp onion powder

SAUCE

- 2 tbsp honey
- 2 tbsp balsamic vinegar
- 2 tbsp ketchup
- 4 cloves garlic minced (2 tsp)

INSTRUCTIONS

01 Pat dry chicken breasts.

02 Mix together paprika, onion powder, salt, and pepper in a small bowl. Then rub seasonings on chicken breasts.

03 In another small bowl make the glaze. Combine ketchup, honey, balsamic vinegar, and minced garlic.

04 Add chicken to a resealable plastic bag with half of the glaze, refrigerate and marinate for at least 2 hours.

05 When chicken is ready, preheat the air fryer at 400°F/200°C for 5 minutes.

06 Place the chicken in the air fryer and cook at 380°F/193°C for about 10-15 minutes, turning halfway (and brush on remaining glaze), until cooked through and instant read thermometer inserted into center of thickest part reads 160°F/71°C. Total time will depend on the thickness of your chicken. Let the chicken rest in the basket for about 5 minutes to finish cooking and redistribute juices.

Blackened Chicken with Avocado Cream Sauce

This low carb air fryer recipe for blackened chicken with avocado cream sauce is full of flavor! Ready in less than 30 minutes AND healthy!

PREP TIME: 10 minutes   **COOK TIME:** 15 minutes   **TOTAL TIME:** 25 minutes   **SERVES:** 4

RECIPE INGREDIENTS

CHICKEN

- 1 1/2 pounds boneless skinless chicken breasts about an inch thick
- 1 tsp paprika
- 1 tsp ground cumin
- 1 tsp onion powder
- 1 tsp pepper
- 1/2 tsp salt
- pinch cayenne pepper, add up to 1/2 tsp for more heat

AVOCADO SAUCE

- 1/2 avocado, chopped
- 1/3 c plain Greek yogurt
- 1 tbsp lemon juice
- 1/2 tsp garlic powder
- 1/8 tsp salt
- 1/8 tsp pepper

INSTRUCTIONS

01. Add paprika, cumin, onion powder, pepper, salt, and cayenne to a gallon resealable plastic bag and shake to combine. Then add the chicken breasts to the bag with the spices and shake to coat chicken evenly.

02. Lightly spray basket with avocado oil.

03. Place the chicken in the air fryer and cook at 380°F/193°C for about 10-15 minutes, turning halfway, until cooked through and instant read thermometer inserted into center of thickest part reads 160°F/71°C. Total time will depend on the thickness of your chicken. Let the chicken rest in the basket for about 5 minutes to finish cooking and redistribute juices.

Curried Chicken

Chicken Curry in the air fryer? You know it!

PREP TIME: 10 minutes   **COOK TIME:** 15 minutes   **TOTAL TIME:** 25 minutes   **SERVES:** 4

RECIPE INGREDIENTS

- ✓ 1/2 -1 lb chicken, cubed
- ✓ 2 tomatoes, sliced in half
- ✓ 1/2 medium onion, cut in wedges
- ✓ 1 tsp ginger, grated
- ✓ 1 tsp garlic, minced
- ✓ 1 tbsp salted butter
- ✓ 2 tsp curry powder
- ✓ 1/2 tsp ground cumin
- ✓ 1/2 tsp ground coriander
- ✓ 1/4 tsp smoked paprika (plus a little more)
- ✓ 1/3 tsp chili powder
- ✓ 2/3 cup heavy cream
- ✓ chopped fresh coriander, for topping

INSTRUCTIONS

SAUCE

01 With an air fryer cake barrel or other similar oven-safe dish, place the tomatoes (sliced side up) and onion. Lightly spray with avocado or olive oil and cook at 320°F/160°C for 25 minutes, or until soft and charred.

02 Once the tomatoes and onions are cooked, add and mix in the garlic, ginger, butter, curry powder, cumin, coriander, smoked paprika, and chili powder. Cook for an additional 5 minutes in the air fryer.

03 Add heavy cream and puree everything together using an immersion blender or food processor. Cover and set aside.

CHICKEN

01 Place the cubed chicken in the air fryer basket. Lightly spray the chicken with oil and sprinkle with paprika. Cook in the air fryer at 380°F/190°C for 5-8 minutes, or until cooked through to 165°F/74°C.

02 Add the chicken to the sauce, stir gently to coat and return the pan to the air fryer for 3-5 minutes or so, until everything is nicely warmed up.

03 Serve with rice and/or naan.

Quick Pizza Stuffed Chicken Thighs

Quick-and-easy air fryer recipe that will please everyone!

PREP TIME: 12 minutes   **COOK TIME:** 14 minutes   **TOTAL TIME:** 26 minutes   **SERVES:** 8

RECIPE INGREDIENTS

- 4-5 boneless skinless chicken thighs
- 1/2 c pizza sauce
- 14 slices turkey pepperoni
- 1/2 small red onion sliced
- 5 oz sliced mozzarella cheese
- 1/2 c shredded Italian blend cheese

INSTRUCTIONS

01. Place trimmed chicken thighs flat in between two pieces of parchment paper, plastic wrap or even wax paper.

02. Pound the chicken to create a thin even piece (to make chicken easier to fold and cook evenly).

03. Evenly spread a spoonful of pizza sauce on each piece of chicken.

04. Place cheese, 2-4 pieces of pepperoni, and onion slices on top of the sauce.

05. Optional, season with Italian seasoning, to your liking.

06. Fold one side of the chicken over onto the other and hold the chicken together with a toothpick (it stays together on its own once it's cooked).

07. Preheat the air fryer at 400°F/200°C for 5 minutes.

08. Place parchment paper in the air fryer basket, (optional: helps catch melted cheese), and set chicken in the air fryer to cook at 380°F/193°C for about 10-15 minutes, turning halfway (and brush on remaining glaze), until cooked through and instant read thermometer inserted into center of thickest part reads 160°F/71°C. Total time will depend on the thickness of your chicken. Add cheese to the top of the chicken during the last minute or two of cooking. Let the chicken rest in the basket for about 5 minutes to finish cooking and redistribute juices.

Copycat Chick-Fil-A Chicken

Say goodbye to expensive chicken strips from Chick-Fil-A!
Enjoy these tasty and simple chicken strips in your air fryer instead.
You will be surprised how much they taste like the real deal!

PREP TIME: 70 minutes   **COOK TIME:** 12 minutes   **TOTAL TIME:** 82 minutes   **SERVES:** 4

RECIPE INGREDIENTS

- 1 lb chicken tenders
- 1 cup dill pickle juice
- 1 large egg
- 1/4 c milk
- 1 1/2 c all-purpose flour
- 1 1/2 tbsp confectioner's sugar
- 1 1/2 tsp paprika
- 3/4 tsp salt
- 3/4 tsp pepper
- 3/4 tsp dried basil
- 3/4 tsp garlic powder
- 3/4 tsp onion powder
- 3/4 tsp celery powder or celery seed - optional

COPYCAT CHICK-FIL-A SAUCE

- 1/4 c mayonnaise
- 2 tbsp honey
- 1 tbsp Dijon mustard
- 1 tbsp yellow mustard
- 2 tsp fresh lemon juice or bottle lemon juice
- 2 tbsp barbecue sauce
- 1/4 tsp salt

INSTRUCTIONS

01 Place the chicken tenders in a resealable plastic bag, add the pickle juice, and refrigerate for an hour (or longer for a stronger pickle flavor). If you are in a pinch for time, refrigerate for only 30 minutes.

02 In a shallow bowl, whisk together the egg and milk.

03 In a second shallow bowl or plate, combine the flour, sugar, paprika, salt, pepper, basil, garlic powder, onion powder and celery powder.

04 Preheat the air fryer to 340°F/170°C for 3 minutes.

05 Remove the chicken from the marinade and pat dry with paper towels.

06 Dredge the chicken in the egg mixture, then in the flour mixture. Place the chicken in a lightly sprayed air fryer basket. Repeat with remaining chicken tenders.

07 Spray the tops of the chicken, cook in the air fryer at 340°F/170°C for 8 minutes, flipping when there is about 2 minutes left.

08 Check the internal temperature of the chicken. My chicken strips were very thin, so this was plenty of time. If yours are thicker, they may need a couple of extra minutes. Add time as needed, making sure to flip the chicken so that each of the sides cook evenly.

FOR THE CHICK FIL A SAUCE:

01 Mix together all the ingredients until well combined.

09 Once the chicken reaches an internal temperature of 155°F/68°C, increase the heat to 400°F/200°C and cook for an additional 2-3 minutes, or until the chicken is crisped to your liking and cooked through.

10 Enjoy with Chick fil a dipping sauce!

Flavorful Greek Chicken Souvlaki

Homemade and tasty Greek chicken souvlaki is super easy in the air fryer. Serve this dish in minutes with a flavorful tzatziki sauce and this recipe will be one of your new favorites!

PREP TIME: 135 minutes   **COOK TIME:** 8 minutes   **TOTAL TIME:** 143 minutes   **SERVES:** 4

RECIPE INGREDIENTS

CHICKEN

- 6-8 oz boneless, skinless chicken breasts cut into bite sized pieces (I used 1 large chicken breast)
- 2 tbsp avocado oil
- 1 tbsp lemon juice
- 1 clove garlic minced
- 1/2 tsp dried oregano
- 1/4 tsp salt

TZATZIKI SAUCE

- 3 oz plain Greek yogurt
- 1/4 cucumber peeled, seeded, and grated
- 1/2 tbsp olive oil
- 1 tsp white vinegar
- 1/2 clove garlic minced
- 1/2 pinch salt

SERVE WITH

- pita bread
- red onions thinly sliced
- tomatoes sliced
- cucumbers sliced
- Kalamata olives
- feta cheese

INSTRUCTIONS

01. Place the marinade ingredients in a resealable plastic bag, seal and shake. Add the chicken, transfer to refrigerator and marinate for 2 hours.

02. Make the tzatziki sauce by mixing together all the ingredients. Place in a bowl and store in the fridge for 1-2 hours.

03. Thread the chicken onto skewers, place in the air fryer basket or on the skewer rack. Cook at 380°F/193°C for 5 minutes. Increase heat to 400°F/200°C for another minute or 2, or until chicken reaches 165°F/74°F.

04. Remove the skewers from the air fryer basket.

05. Assemble grilled chicken souvlaki pitas. First, spread Tzatziki sauce on the pita, slide chicken pieces off skewers with a fork and then add veggies, olives, and feta. Enjoy!

RECIPE NOTES

You can find air fryer skewers at AirFryerTools. com. OR just spread cubed chicken on the bottom of the air fryer basket to cook.

Hibachi Style Chicken with Yum Yum Sauce

*Simple, quick, and easy hibachi style chicken with Yum Yum sauce
is a delicious and flavorful meal you will love!*

PREP TIME: 10 minutes   **COOK TIME:** 15 minutes   **TOTAL TIME:** 25 minutes   **SERVES:** 4

RECIPE INGREDIENTS

HIBACHI CHICKEN

- 2 raw chicken breast cut into bite sized pieces
- 1 small onion cut into slices
- 8 oz mushrooms cut into fourths
- 2 small zucchini cut into bite sized pieces
- 1/2 tsp ground ginger
- 1/4 tsp black pepper
- 1 tbsp garlic powder
- 1/4 c soy sauce
- 2 tbsp olive oil

YUM YUM SAUCE

- 1 c mayonnaise
- 1/4 c water
- 1 tsp tomato paste or ketchup
- 1 tbsp melted butter
- 1/2 tsp garlic powder
- 1 tsp sugar
- 1/4 tsp paprika

INSTRUCTIONS

01. Preheat the air fryer to 400°F/200°C for 5 minutes.

02. Cut up the chicken and vegetables.

03. Toss with 2 tbsp of olive oil and seasoning mix.

04. Place the chicken, vegetables and seasoning into the preheated air fryer basket.

05. Cook at 380°F/193°C for 12-15 minutes. Stir at the halfway point.

06. While the chicken is cooking, make the Yum Yum sauce. Mix all the sauce ingredients together in a bowl until well combined.

07. Once the chicken is cooked (reaches an internal temperature of 165°F/74°F), Transfer chicken and vegetables to a serving bowl or individual plates and enjoy with the Yum Yum sauce!

Balsamic Chicken and Veggies

This tasty, flavorful, fresh dinner idea is a huge hit in my home!
I love that it's an all-in-one dinner!

PREP TIME: 25 minutes   **COOK TIME:** 17 minutes   **TOTAL TIME:** 42 minutes   **SERVES:** 8

RECIPE INGREDIENTS

- 2 small zucchini squash
- 2 small yellow squash
- 1 bell pepper
- 1 head of broccoli (about 4 cups chopped)
- 1 small red onion
- 1 1/2 lbs chicken
- 1-2 c cherry or grape tomatoes, halved

MARINADE

- 1/3 c balsamic vinegar
- 3 tbsp olive or avocado oil
- 1-2 tbsp honey
- 1 tsp dried basil
- 1/2 tsp dried oregano
- 1 tsp coarse kosher salt
- 1/2 tsp pepper

INSTRUCTIONS

01 Chop veggies & chicken into bite sized pieces and stir together in a large bowl.

02 In a separate bowl, blend marinade together.

03 Stir marinade into veggies & chicken and marinate for 15 minutes–2 hours.

04 Cook half the batch for 370°F/187°C for 12 minutes (stirring once at halfway point).

05 Cook for 5 more minutes at 400°F/200°C or until chicken registers 165°F/74°F & veggies have reached your desired tenderness.

Honey Garlic Chicken and Veggies

I love this easy, healthy dinner recipe! One-pan chicken and veggies with a simple, delicious honey garlic marinade!

PREP TIME: 15 minutes   **COOK TIME:** 25 minutes   **TOTAL TIME:** 40 minutes   **SERVES:** 4

RECIPE INGREDIENTS

- 3 tbsp honey
- 3 cloves garlic minced
- 1 tbsp low-sodium soy sauce or coconut aminos
- 1/8 tsp salt
- 1/8 tsp black pepper
- 1 lb chicken breast or tenderloins
- 4 medium red potatoes, washed and cubed into bite size pieces
- 2 c fresh broccoli florets, washed and chopped into bite size pieces
- 1-2 tbsp avocado oil

INSTRUCTIONS

01. In a 4 quart bowl, whisk the marinade ingredients together. Set chicken inside bowl and stir to coat. Let chicken marinate while you prep the veggies.

02. Place veggies in air fryer basket and stir in 1-2 tbsp of oil, coating veggies.

03. Place chicken over veggies and pour remaining glaze over chicken and veggies.

04. Air fry at 360°F/182°C for 14 minutes, flipping chicken once and stirring vegetables midway.

05. Remove chicken at internal temperature of 165°F/74°F, and tent chicken with foil or a clean bowl.

06. Cook veggies for another 5-8 minutes at 350°F/176°C until potatoes are tender and veggies are done to your liking.

Quick Chicken and Veggies

You'll love how quick and easy it is to cook up healthy chicken and veggies in your air fryer! Only 10 minutes to cook!

PREP TIME: 25 minutes   **COOK TIME:** 17 minutes   **TOTAL TIME:** 42 minutes   **SERVES:** 8

RECIPE INGREDIENTS

- ☑ 1 lb boneless skinless chicken breast cut into bite-size pieces
- ☑ 10-12 oz frozen veggie mix
- ☑ 1 tbsp olive or avocado oil
- ☑ 2 garlic cloves minced
- ☑ 1/2 tsp garlic powder
- ☑ 1/2 tsp chili powder
- ☑ 1/2 tsp salt
- ☑ 1/2 tsp pepper
- ☑ 1 tbsp Italian seasoning
- ☑ lemon wedges, optional

INSTRUCTIONS

01 Preheat air fryer to 400°F/200°C.

02 Add chicken and veggies to a large bowl and drizzle oil over top. Sprinkle on seasonings. Stir to coat chicken and veggies evenly.

03 Transfer mixture to air fryer. Cook at 400°F/200°C for 10 minutes, shaking halfway through, or until charred and cooked through. Serve with lemon wedges if desired.

RECIPE NOTES

Make your own veggie mix with fresh broccoli florets, chopped zucchini, chopped bell pepper, and onion.

Hawaiian Chicken and Coconut Rice

This Hawaiian chicken is the best and one of our most favorite summer recipes.
With bold, juicy flavors, you will love this recipe too!

PREP TIME: 10 minutes   **COOK TIME:** 16 minutes   **TOTAL TIME:** 26 minutes   **SERVES:** 4

RECIPE INGREDIENTS

CHICKEN

- 3 lbs chicken thighs, boned, trimmed and halved
- 1 c soy sauce
- 1 c brown sugar
- 1/2 bunch green onions thinly sliced
- 1 garlic clove minced
- 1 tsp sesame oil
- 13.6 oz can coconut milk

VEGETABLES & PINEAPPLE

- 1 red bell pepper sliced
- 1 zucchini sliced on the diagonal
- 1/2 fresh pineapple sliced

COCONUT RICE

- 2 cups jasmine rice
- 13.6 oz can coconut milk
- 1/2 c water
- 1 tsp Kosher salt

INSTRUCTIONS

01. Trim the chicken and prepare the vegetables and pineapple.

02. In a bowl, mix together the soy sauce, brown sugar, green onions, garlic, oil, and coconut milk.

03. Remove 1 cup of the marinade for the vegetables.

04. Place the chicken and the vegetables/ pineapple in their respective marinades and refrigerate for at least 1 hour. You can marinate overnight and up to 24 hours.

05. When you are ready to make dinner, start with your rice. For the coconut rice: in a medium-large pot, bring the coconut milk and water to a boil. Add the salt and rice. Stir together and turn the heat to low. Cover and cook for 15 minutes, stirring at the halfway point. Remove from heat and let it rest for 5 minutes.

06. For the chicken: Lightly spray the air fryer basket with oil and place half of the chicken inside in a single layer. Discard chicken marinade.

07. Cook at 380°F/193°C for 16 minutes.

08. At the halfway point, flip the chicken over and add half of the vegetables.

09 Cook until the chicken registers 165°F/74°C with an instant read thermometer. Repeat for the remaining chicken and vegetables. (If your air fryer has room to hold everything in one batch, go for it! Just don't overcrowd the air fryer basket).

10 Serve over the coconut rice.

TO MAKE AHEAD

01 Place the marinade ingredients in a resealable plastic bag and shake to combine. Add the pineapple, vegetables, and chicken. Seal, pressing out excess air. Place flat in the freezer.

02 Pull out the night before and place it in a bowl in the refrigerator, so that it doesn't leak in the fridge. When you are ready to cook in the air fryer, dump out the marinade in a bowl through a strainer. Then place the chicken, vegetables, and pineapple in the air fryer basket and cook for 16 minutes at 380°F/193°C, flip at the halfway point.

Fast Kielbasa Veggie Dinner

This turkey kielbasa veggie dinner is terrific for those busy nights!
Mix it up with your favorite veggies!

PREP TIME: 10 minutes **COOK TIME:** 14 minutes **TOTAL TIME:** 24 minutes **SERVES:** 4

RECIPE INGREDIENTS

- 12 oz turkey kielbasa cut on the diagonal into 1/2-inch-thick slices
- 1/2 -1 pound asparagus trimmed, cut into 2-inch pieces
- 4 oz grape tomatoes halved
- 1 orange bell pepper cut into 2-inch pieces
- 1/2 tbsp avocado oil
- 1/2 tsp sea salt
- 3/4 tsp Italian seasoning
- 1 tsp paprika
- 1/2 tsp garlic powder
- 1/4 tsp black pepper

INSTRUCTIONS

01 Cut and prepare the asparagus, peppers, kielbasa, and tomatoes.

02 Combine asparagus, peppers, and kielbasa in a bowl, and stir in about a 1/2 tbsp avocado oil.

03 Blend sea salt, Italian seasoning, paprika, garlic powder, and black pepper together.

04 Add seasonings to the asparagus, peppers and kielbasa mixture and stir well.

05 Pour the mixture in the air fryer basket and cook for 12 minutes at 380°F/193°C, stirring half way through cooking. Add tomatoes and cook for 2 minutes more.

06 Remove from the air fryer basket and enjoy!

Easy Chicken Fajitas

Easy, quick, and delicious! We love chicken fajitas
and I love that it's on the table in less than 30 minutes

PREP TIME: 5 minutes   **COOK TIME:** 16 minutes   **TOTAL TIME:** 21 minutes   **SERVES:** 4

RECIPE INGREDIENTS

- 1 lb boneless skinless chicken sliced
- 12 oz bag frozen peppers and onion
- 1 tbsp oil
- 1 packet fajita seasoning or homemade fajita seasoning (see notes)

INSTRUCTIONS

01 Place sliced chicken and frozen veggies in a mixing bowl. Drizzle oil over all and stir to coat.

02 Sprinkle fajita seasoning over all, stir to coat evenly.

03 Place mixture into air fryer basket and cook at 360°F/182°C for 8 minutes. Stir contents.

04 Cook for an additional 5-8 minutes until chicken is done and reaches internal temperature of 165°F/74°C.

05 Serve warm with tortillas or on a salad with your favorite fajita toppings, like cheese, cilantro, sour cream, avocado, guacamole, etc.

Chicken Shepherd's Pie

An easy and delicious way to enjoy leftover chicken
with this spin on the traditional Shepherd's Pie!

PREP TIME: 5 minutes   **COOK TIME:** 17 minutes   **TOTAL TIME:** 22 minutes   **SERVES:** 4

RECIPE INGREDIENTS

- 2 (6-oz) boneless, skinless chicken breasts
- 1/4 tsp salt, plus extra for sprinkling
- 1/4 tsp black pepper plus extra for sprinkling
- 12 oz jar chicken gravy
- 1 1/2 cup frozen mixed vegetables, thawed
- 1/2 tsp onion powder
- 2 cups prepared mashed potatoes
- 2 tbsp butter, melted

RECIPE NOTES

This recipe is great with leftover Thanksgiving foods or even leftover chicken!

INSTRUCTIONS

01 Preheat the air fryer to 350°F/176°C for 5 minutes.

02 Coat the air fryer basket with cooking spray. Sprinkle chicken with salt and pepper, place in the basket, and air fry for 5 minutes. Turn chicken over and continue to cook 5 to 6 more minutes or until no pink remains in the center. Remove to a cutting board, let cool slightly, and cut into 1/2-inch chunks.

03 Meanwhile, in a skillet over medium heat, combine gravy, vegetables, onion powder, 1/4 tsp salt, and 1/4 tsp pepper. Cook 5 to 7 minutes or until heated through. When chicken is ready, stir that in and spoon mixture evenly into 4 (1-c) ramekins.

04 Top each ramekin with 1/2 cup mashed potatoes and drizzle melted butter on top.

05 Place ramekins in the basket and cook for 6 to 7 minutes at 400°F/200°C or until heated through and the tops are golden.

BBQ Chicken Stuffed Sweet Potatoes

Bursting with fresh flavors, this meal is one you won't regret trying.

PREP TIME: 5 minutes   **COOK TIME:** 40 minutes   **TOTAL TIME:** 45 minutes   **SERVES:** 2

RECIPE INGREDIENTS

- ✔ 2 sweet potatoes
- ✔ 1/2 lb chicken cut into bite size pieces
- ✔ 1/2 -1 bell pepper cut into bite size pieces
- ✔ 1/2 c red onion cut into bite size pieces
- ✔ 1/2 c frozen corn
- ✔ 1/2 c black beans
- ✔ 1/2 tbsp oil of choice
- ✔ 1/2 tsp salt
- ✔ 1/2 tsp ground cumin
- ✔ 1/2 tsp brown sugar
- ✔ 1/2 tsp paprika
- ✔ 1/4 tsp chili powder
- ✔ sprinkle black pepper

TOPPINGS

- ✔ avocado
- ✔ cherry tomatoes
- ✔ BBQ sauce mixed with Greek yogurt or sour cream
- ✔ cilantro

INSTRUCTIONS

01. Wash and scrub your sweet potatoes so they are clean and free from dirt. Pierce with a fork, 4-5 times. Rub oil on the potatoes. Place in the air fryer basket and sprinkle with salt. Cook at 380°F/193°C for 35 minutes.

02. In a bowl, combine the chicken, corn, bell pepper, red onion, black beans with the oil and seasonings.

03. When there is 15 minutes left on the timer, add the chicken and veggies to the air fryer basket.

04. When there are 7 minutes left, stir the veggies and check on the chicken and sweet potatoes. Chicken needs to register at 165°F/74°C. The cooking time really depends on the size of your potatoes, so you will just have to watch it carefully. Adjust the time as needed.

05. Once the sweet potatoes are easily pierced with a knife and chicken has finished cooking, remove the sweet potatoes from the air fryer basket. Cut open the sweet potato and top with veggies, chicken, toppings, and enjoy!

'Southern' Fried Chicken

The healthiest and crispiest Southern fried chicken,
courtesy of your air fryer!

PREP TIME: 150 minutes   **COOK TIME:** 30 minutes   **TOTAL TIME:** 180 minutes   **SERVES:** 4

RECIPE INGREDIENTS

- 1 1/2 c buttermilk (see substitution on page 248)
- 1/4 c hot sauce
- 1 tbsp smoked paprika
- 1 tbsp onion powder
- 1 tbsp garlic powder
- 1 tbsp salt
- 1 tbsp pepper
- 2-3 pounds chicken drumsticks (about 8 drumsticks)
- 1 1/2 c flour
- 1/2 c cornstarch, (if you don't have cornstarch, use a 1/2 cup of flour or almond flour)
- 1 tsp baking powder
- avocado oil

RECIPE NOTES

Works with chicken breasts, wings, thighs or boneless tenders. Adjust cooking time according to size of meat and be sure to check the internal temperature reaches 165F.

INSTRUCTIONS

01 Mix the smoked paprika, onion powder, garlic powder, salt, and pepper together in a small bowl.

02 Make the brine: whisk together hot sauce, buttermilk, and half of the spice mixture.

03 Combine drumsticks and brine in a resealable plastic bag. Marinate, refrigerated, for at least 1-2 hours or overnight.

04 Make the dredge: combine flour, cornstarch, baking powder, and the rest of the spices in a plastic bag and shake to mix everything together.

05 After the chicken has finished soaking, add up to 3 drumsticks at a time into the dredge bag. Coat the drumsticks by shaking the bag. Take the drumsticks out of the bag and set on a plate. Repeat this for all the drumsticks.

06 Pour the remaining buttermilk mixture from the brine bag into a bowl and double dredge the drumsticks in the brine and then in the dredge.

07 Let the drumsticks rest for 10 minutes.

08 Preheat the air fryer to 400°F/200°C for 5 minutes.

09 Spray the drumsticks with oil to help the dredge adhere to the chicken. This will also help crisp the chicken.

10 Spray the air fryer basket with oil and place 4 drumsticks to the basket.

11 Cook for 15 minutes at 380°F/193°C, flipping once at the halfway point.

The Best Chicken Tenders

These air fried chicken tenders are covered in a crispy, flavorful breading, and each bite is juicy and delicious.

PREP TIME: 35 minutes   **COOK TIME:** 12 minutes   **TOTAL TIME:** 47 minutes   **SERVES:** 4

RECIPE INGREDIENTS

- ✓ 1 1/2 lbs chicken tenders, about 12 tenders
- ✓ 1/2 c buttermilk (see substitution on page 248)
- ✓ 1/2 c panko
- ✓ 1/2 c flour
- ✓ 1 tsp paprika
- ✓ 1/2 tsp celery seed
- ✓ 1/2 tsp ground ginger
- ✓ 1/2 tsp salt
- ✓ 1/2 tsp ground black pepper
- ✓ 1/4 tsp garlic powder
- ✓ 1/4 tsp dried thyme
- ✓ 1/4 tsp dried oregano
- ✓ 1/4 tsp baking powder
- ✓ 1/8 tsp cayenne (optional)
- ✓ avocado or olive oil spray

INSTRUCTIONS

01. Place the chicken tenders in a resealable plastic bag and pour the buttermilk into the bag. Let marinate in the refrigerator for 30 minutes.

02. In a shallow bowl combine the panko, flour, baking powder, and spices.

03. Remove the chicken strips from the buttermilk with a fork, shake off excess buttermilk, and dredge in the breadcrumb mixture to coat on all sides.

04. Put the chicken fingers in a lightly sprayed air fryer basket. Then lightly spray with your favorite oil and cook at 370°F/187°C for 10-12 minutes, flipping halfway through, until the internal temperature reads 165°F/74°C and the chicken tenders are golden brown and crispy.

Crunchy Popcorn Chicken

Enjoy this quick air fryer popcorn chicken that has NO oil!

PREP TIME: 10 minutes   **COOK TIME:** 10 minutes   **TOTAL TIME:** 20 minutes   **SERVES:** 8

RECIPE INGREDIENTS

- 1 lb uncooked chicken breasts or tenders cut into 36–40 cubes
- 1/2–1 c cornstarch
- 1 1/2 c coconut milk
- 1 1/2 tsp pickle juice or vinegar
- 4–6 c finely crushed corn flakes
- 1 tsp garlic powder
- 1 tsp onion powder
- 1 tsp paprika
- 1/2 tsp pepper
- 1/4 tsp salt optional
- pinch cayenne pepper, **optional**

INSTRUCTIONS

01 Mix together coconut milk and pickle juice.

02 In a resealable plastic bag, finely crush cornflakes together with all the seasoning powders.

03 Place cornstarch in a shallow bowl or plate, the crushed mixture in another shallow bowl or plate and the coconut milk in a third bowl.

04 Coat each chicken piece in cornstarch, then the coconut liquid, and roll in the corn flakes.

05 Repeat for each chicken piece and place them evenly in the air fryer.

06 Cook at 400°F/200°C for 8-10 minutes or until chicken is cooked to 165°F/74°C. Flip chicken halfway through cooking.

20 Minute Crispy Chicken Parmesan

*Easy chicken parmesan in the air fryer that
everyone will love and ready in just 20 minutes.*

PREP TIME: 8 minutes   **COOK TIME:** 12 minutes   **TOTAL TIME:** 20 minutes   **SERVES:** 4

RECIPE INGREDIENTS

- 4 small chicken breasts or 8 chicken tenders
- 1/2 c panko
- 1/2 c parmesan cheese
- 1 tsp onion powder
- 1 tsp garlic powder
- 1 tsp Italian seasoning
- 2 eggs, beaten
- 1/2 tsp salt
- 1/4 tsp pepper
- 1 c flour
- favorite pasta or tomato sauce
- mozzarella cheese fresh or shredded

INSTRUCTIONS

01. Combine panko, parmesan, onion powder, garlic powder, and Italian seasoning. Spread in a shallow dish.

02. Place flour in a shallow bowl or dish. Pour beaten eggs into a second shallow dish.

03. Place dishes in a row starting with flour, then eggs and finally crumb mixture.

04. Pat dry the chicken, pound it to even thickness with a meat pounder, then season both sides with salt and pepper.

05. Dip the chicken in flour, next the egg, then the panko mixture. Make sure to coat both sides.

06. Spray air fryer basket with oil. Place chicken in the air fryer in a single layer, leaving enough room between the chicken so air can flow through. Spray the top of chicken with oil.

07. Cook at 350°F/176°C for 8 minutes turning chicken halfway through.

08. With instant read food thermometer, make sure the internal temperature is around 160-165°F/71-74°C. If not, cook for an additional minute or two.

09. Top each piece of chicken with 2 tbsp of pasta or tomato sauce and a slice of mozzarella.

10. Cook for an additional 3 minutes at 380°F/193°C or until the cheese is melted.

Crispy Potato Chip Chicken

Wondering what to do with those leftover chips that no one is eating?
Make this delicious potato chip chicken in the air fryer!
So flavorful and crunchy, especially for only 5-ingredients!

PREP TIME: 5 minutes   **COOK TIME:** 15 minutes   **TOTAL TIME:** 20 minutes   **SERVES:** 4

RECIPE INGREDIENTS

- 1 lb Chicken cutlets or tenders
- 2 eggs
- 1 c crushed potato chips, any flavour
- 1 tbsp mixed herbs (dried oregano, sage, onion powder, Italian seasoning etc.)

INSTRUCTIONS

01 Spray air fryer basket with non-stick cooking spray.

02 Beat eggs in shallow bowl.

03 Crush chips with seasonings in a resealable plastic bag.

04 Dip chicken in egg coating all sides, then coat in chips patting gently to adhere.

05 Place chicken in basket and cook at 380°F/193°C for about 10-15 minutes, turning halfway, until cooked through and instant read thermometer inserted into center of thickest part reads 160°F/71°C and coating is crispy. Total time will depend on the thickness of your chicken. Let the chicken rest in the basket for about 5 minutes to finish cooking and redistribute juices.

Ritz Cracker Chicken

Make quick, easy, and delicious chicken tenders with Ritz© crackers!
You will be surprised to find just how tasty and simple this meal actually is!

PREP TIME: 6 minutes   **COOK TIME:** 10 minutes   **TOTAL TIME:** 16 minutes   **SERVES:** 5

RECIPE INGREDIENTS

- 3 pounds chicken tender cut into pieces
- 2 sleeves Ritz© crackers crushed
- 1 tsp Italian seasoning
- 1/2 tsp Creole seasoning (see substitution on page 248)
- 1/2 tsp dried parsley
- 1/2 tsp rosemary chopped
- 3 eggs
- 1 tbsp Worcestershire sauce
- 1 1/2 cups parmesan cheese, grated

INSTRUCTIONS

01 Cut the chicken into smaller pieces.

02 In a shallow bowl, mix the eggs with the Worcestershire sauce. Set aside.

03 Crush the 2 sleeves of crackers, place in shallow dish. Add the seasonings and herbs. Mix together until combined.

04 Place the parmesan cheese in its own shallow dish.

05 Spray air fryer basket with avocado oil. Dip the chicken in the egg, cheese, then cracker crumbles. Place in air fryer and repeat.

06 Spray the tops of the chicken with avocado oil.

07 Cook at 380°F/193°C for 7-8 minutes (or until the chicken registers at 165°F/74°C), flipping the chicken at the halfway point.

Honey Mustard Chicken

This honey mustard chicken recipe is incredibly easy and quick, not to mention delicious!

PREP TIME: 15 minutes   **COOK TIME:** 12 minutes   **TOTAL TIME:** 27 minutes   **SERVES:** 4-6

RECIPE INGREDIENTS

- ✓ 2 tbsp butter
- ✓ 1/4 c honey
- ✓ 1/4 c Dijon Mustard
- ✓ 1 tbsp avocado oil
- ✓ 2 tsp fresh lemon juice
- ✓ salt and pepper
- ✓ 4 boneless skinless chicken breasts

INSTRUCTIONS

01 Melt butter in the microwave or on the stovetop. Stir in the honey, Dijon mustard, olive oil, and lemon juice. Season with salt and pepper to taste.

02 Transfer about half of the honey mustard mixture to a separate bowl for later.

03 Pound down the chicken for a more even thickness, about 1 inch thick.

04 Brush both sides of the chicken with honey mustard glaze and then place it inside air fryer basket.

05 Cook at 380°F/193°C for 11-12 minutes, flipping at the halfway point.

06 Pull the chicken out once it reaches about 160°F/71°C and tent it in tinfoil to finish cooking and reach an internal temp of 165°F/74°C.

07 Top with remaining glaze and enjoy!

BBQ Chicken Burritos

If you don't count the time it takes to cook the chicken (pst... use leftovers!)
this is a super fast delicious meal to throw together!
It's a great alternative to taco night and a family favorite!

PREP TIME: 15 minutes   **COOK TIME:** 5 minutes   **TOTAL TIME:** 20 minutes   **SERVES:** 6

RECIPE INGREDIENTS

- 1 lb chicken, cooked and shredded
- 1 can black beans, rinsed and drained
- 1 c frozen corn, thawed
- 1 c BBQ sauce
- splash of lime juice
- fresh chopped cilantro, optional

INSTRUCTIONS

01. Mix together the ingredients in a bowl.

02. Add a spoonful of the mixture over a tortilla.

03. Roll the tortilla into thirds and lightly mist with oil.

04. Place in the air fryer basket and cook at 350°F/175°C for 5 minutes, flipping at the halfway point. Or cook until food and tortilla reaches desired crispiness.

BBQ Chicken Wings

Make perfectly cooked chicken wings in the air fryer – straight from frozen, with almost no prep time, and less cooking time than in the oven!

PREP TIME: 2 minutes   **COOK TIME:** 40 minutes   **TOTAL TIME:** 42 minutes   **SERVES:** 4

RECIPE INGREDIENTS

- frozen chicken wings – up to 2 lbs depending on size of basket
- garlic salt to taste
- pepper to taste
- BBQ or wing sauce to taste (see homemade BBQ Sauce recipe on page 249)

INSTRUCTIONS

01. Dump frozen chicken wings into air fryer basket. It's ok if they overlap because they will shrink as they cook. The amount you can cook at once will depend on the size of your air fryer.

02. Cook at 350°F/176°C for 10 minutes to thaw. Carefully pour out any excess liquid.

03. Season both sides of chicken with garlic salt and pepper.

04. Cook at 380°F/193°C for 25 minutes, flipping halfway through cooking time.

05. Coat chicken with your favorite sauce.

06. Cook at 400°F/200°C for 5 minutes until wings are glazed and cooked to 165°F/74°C internal temperature. Serve warm and enjoy!

FISH

NOTES

Coconut Shrimp with Piña Colada Dipping Sauce

This coconut shrimp is easy and delicious! Especially with this copycat piña colada dipping sauce. Give it a try!

PREP TIME: 20 minutes   **COOK TIME:** 8 minutes   **TOTAL TIME:** 28 minutes   **SERVES:** 5

RECIPE INGREDIENTS

COCONUT SHRIMP

- 1 pound raw jumbo shrimp peeled and deveined, tails-on
- salt and pepper
- 2/3 c all-purpose flour
- 2 large eggs, lightly beaten
- 1/3 c panko
- 1/3 c unsweetened coconut

PIÑA COLADA DIPPING SAUCE

- 1/2 c sour cream
- 1/2 c canned cream of coconut like Coco Lopez
- 2 tbsp crushed pineapple drained
- 1/2 tsp fresh lemon juice

INSTRUCTIONS

01. Pat shrimp dry with paper towels, then lightly season with salt and pepper.

02. In a shallow bowl, mix together flour, 1/2 tsp salt, and 1/4 tsp pepper. In a second bowl, add a pinch of salt to the lightly beaten eggs. In a third shallow bowl, mix together panko and coconut.

03. Coat each shrimp in flour mixture, gently shaking off excess. Then dip into the eggs and let excess drip off. Dredge in the coconut/panko mixture and gently press to coat. Transfer to a large plate or platter until all shrimp are coated.

04. Preheat the air fryer to 380°F/193°C for 5 minutes. Spray basket with oil spray. Place shrimp in a single layer in the basket, then lightly spray shrimp with oil spray. Cook for about 8 minutes, until golden brown. Flip halfway through cooking time and lightly spray the other side with oil.

05. Transfer to a warm platter for serving and place the bowl of sauce in the middle.

06. For piña colada sauce: Gently stir ingredients together by hand. Do not overmix. If the sour cream starts to break down from mixing too much, the sauce will be too thin.

Quick Tilapia Fish Fry

Enjoy this yummy tilapia in 15 minutes!
It's a quick and easy dinner for everyone!

PREP TIME: 2 minutes   **COOK TIME:** 40 minutes   **TOTAL TIME:** 42 minutes   **SERVES:** 4

RECIPE INGREDIENTS

- ✓ 1 pound tilapia, or other mild white fish
- ✓ 2 eggs
- ✓ 1 package Louisiana fish fry

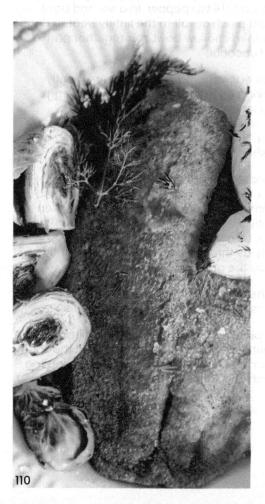

INSTRUCTIONS

01. Preheat the air fryer to 400°F/200°C for 5 minutes.

02. Rinse the tilapia and pat it dry.

03. In a shallow bowl, whisk the eggs until smooth.

04. In a separate shallow bowl or plate, pour out the package of the Louisiana fish fry.

05. Dip the tilapia in the egg wash. Be sure to cover both sides.

06. Then, place the tilapia in the fish fry, turning and patting gently to coat both sides.

07. Spray the air fryer basket with oil. Place the fish in a single layer in the air fryer basket. Spray with oil and cook at 350°F/176°C for 8 minutes.

08. Fish is fully cooked when it registers at 145ºF/63ºC on instant read food thermometer.

09. Enjoy with a dipping sauce of your choice! I loved serving it with a sweet garlic chili sauce.

Honey Mustard Salmon

*Easy and quick, this air fryer honey mustard salmon
will quickly become a family favorite.*

PREP TIME: 5 minutes   **COOK TIME:** 10 minutes   **TOTAL TIME:** 15 minutes   **SERVES:** 3

RECIPE INGREDIENTS

- 3 salmon filets, 1 1/2 inches thick
- salt and pepper, to taste
- 2 tbsp honey
- 1 tbsp Dijon mustard

INSTRUCTIONS

01 Make a foil sling for the air fryer basket, about 4 inches tall and a few inches longer than the width of the basket. Lay foil widthwise across basket, pressing it into and up the sides. Lightly spray foil and basket with cooking spray.

02 Pat salmon dry with paper towels. Season with salt and pepper.

03 In a small bowl, mix together honey and Dijon, until well combined. Reserve 1 tbsp of glaze. Drizzle remaining glaze evenly over salmon fillets, tops and sides.

04 Arrange filets skin side down on sling in the basket, with space between them. (The number of filets you can fit in your air fryer at one time depends on the size of the fillets and the size of your air fryer).

05 Cook at 350°F/176°C for 8-10 minutes, until salmon flakes easily and registers at 145°F/63°C (thinner salmon will be ready sooner, thicker salmon will take more time).

06 Using sling, carefully lift salmon from air fryer. Loosen the skin with a fish spatula or utensil, then transfer fillets to plate, leaving skin behind.

07 Drizzle reserved sauce over fillets. Garnish with fresh parsley, if desired. Serve warm.

RECIPE NOTES

Works with skin-on filets and filets without skin.

Parmesan Crusted Salmon

This incredibly simple dish is packed with flavor
and can be whipped up in less than 15 minutes!

PREP TIME: 5 minutes   **COOK TIME:** 8 minutes   **TOTAL TIME:** 13 minutes   **SERVES:** 2

RECIPE INGREDIENTS

- 2 salmon filets
- 1/4 c mayonnaise
- 1 tsp herb and garlic seasoning
- shredded parmesan cheese, to taste

INSTRUCTIONS

01 Preheat the air fryer at 400°F/200°C for 5 minutes.

02 Mix together the mayonnaise with the herb and garlic seasoning.

03 Pat dry the salmon fillets and place in the air fryer basket.

04 Spread this mixture onto the top of the salmon filets. Top with parmesan cheese.

05 Cook at 350°F/176°C for 8-10 minutes, until salmon flakes easily and registers at 145°F/63°C (thinner salmon will be ready sooner, thicker salmon will take more time).

Honey Garlic Shrimp

*This honey garlic shrimp will quickly become your next
go-to dinner because it is so easy to make and is simply divine.*

PREP TIME: 10 minutes   **COOK TIME:** 6 minutes   **TOTAL TIME:** 16 minutes   **SERVES:** 4

RECIPE INGREDIENTS

- 1 lb uncooked medium or large shrimp, peeled & deveined (fresh or thawed)
- 1/3 c honey
- 1/4 c soy sauce
- 1 tbsp minced garlic
- 1 tsp minced fresh ginger, optional

INSTRUCTIONS

01 Mix all ingredients except shrimp together, reserve half for glazing the shrimp after cooking.

02 Coat shrimp with sauce in a resealable plastic bag or in a large bowl.

03 Preheat air fryer for 5 minutes, then cook shrimp at 370°F/187°C for 6 minutes, stirring halfway through cooking.

04 Pour reserved sauce over shrimp servings once plated.

RECIPE NOTES

If you aren't a fan of a strong garlic taste, I recommend reducing the amount of garlic from 1 tbsp to 2 tsp.

Bang Bang Shrimp

Take this classic bang bang shrimp and spice it up with the air fryer.
This recipe is not only packed with flavor, but it is so easy to make too.

PREP TIME: 10 minutes   **COOK TIME:** 7 minutes   **TOTAL TIME:** 17 minutes   **SERVES:** 4

RECIPE INGREDIENTS

- 1 lb extra-large (26/30 count) raw shrimp peeled and deveined, tails off or on
- 3 tbsp all-purpose flour
- 1 c panko breadcrumbs
- 2 large eggs
- oil spray

THAI SEASONING MIX

- 1 tsp onion powder
- 1 tsp garlic powder
- 3/4 tsp paprika
- 3/4 tsp basil
- 1/2 zest of 1 lime
- 1/2 tsp coriander
- 1/4 tsp salt
- dash of cayenne pepper
- dash of black pepper

BANG BANG SAUCE

- 1/4 c plain Greek yogurt
- 3 tbsp Thai-style sweet chili sauce
- 1 tsp Sriracha sauce, plus more to taste

INSTRUCTIONS

01. Prepare 3 separate shallow bowls. In the first bowl, place the flour. In the second, whisk together the eggs. In the third, mix the panko with the Thai seasoning mix (If you want traditional bang bang shrimp, omit these seasonings and combine the panko with ½ tsp of salt).

02. Dredge the shrimp in the flour, then egg and finally the panko mixture. Lightly spray the air fryer basket. Place shrimp in the air fryer basket in a single layer and lightly spray the top of the shrimp.

03. Cook in the air fryer at 400°F/200°C for 5 minutes. Flip the shrimp and cook for an additional 2-3 minutes, or until it is golden and crispy.

04. While the shrimp is cooking, prepare the bang bang sauce by whisking together the ingredients.

05. Remove the shrimp from the air fryer basket and enjoy while warm!

Shrimp Tacos

*A quick, easy, healthy, and flavorful dinner that everyone
loves AND that is perfect for busy weeknight dinners!*

PREP TIME: 3 minutes   **COOK TIME:** 7 minutes   **TOTAL TIME:** 10 minutes   **SERVES:** 4

RECIPE INGREDIENTS

- ✓ 1 lb small shrimp, raw, peeled, deveined, tails-off
- ✓ 1 tbsp oil
- ✓ 3/4 tsp chili powder
- ✓ 3/4 tsp garlic powder
- ✓ 1/2 tsp cumin powder
- ✓ 1/2 tsp onion powder
- ✓ pinch of salt and pepper

TOPPINGS

- ✓ 4 flour tortillas or corn tortillas
- ✓ green shredded cabbage
- ✓ sliced avocados
- ✓ crumbled cotija cheese or feta cheese
- ✓ cilantro
- ✓ lime wedges

INSTRUCTIONS

01. Toss shrimp with oil, chili powder, garlic powder, cumin, onion powder, salt and pepper in a bowl. Place shrimp in the air fryer basket.

02. Cook at 400°F/200°C for 5-6 minutes or until shrimp is cooked through. For crispier shrimp, cook for an additional minute or two.

03. Assemble tortillas with shrimp, cabbage (optional), and cheese (optional). Place tacos in the air fryer basket and cook at 400°F/200°C for 1 minute to warm tortillas. Cook at 400°F/200°C for 2-3 minutes for crispy taco shells.

04. Remove tacos from the air fryer, add the toppings and serve.

Crab Cakes

Enjoy easy homemade crab cakes in the air fryer!
This recipe is Keto friendly but everyone will enjoy it.

PREP TIME: 40 minutes   **COOK TIME:** 10 minutes   **TOTAL TIME:** 50 minutes   **SERVES:** 4

RECIPE INGREDIENTS

- 2, 6 oz cans lump crab meat, drained
- 1/4 c almond flour
- 2 tbsp chopped fresh parsley
- 1 green onion finely sliced
- 1/2 tsp Old Bay seasoning
- 1/2 tsp salt
- 1/4 tsp pepper
- 1 large egg
- 1 tbsp mayonnaise
- 2 tsp Dijon mustard
- 2 tbsp butter melted

INSTRUCTIONS

01. In a large bowl, stir together the drained crab meat, almond flour, parsley, green onion, Old Bay, salt, and pepper. Crab meat should remain in small lumps. Stir in the egg, mayo, and mustard, until incorporated.

02. Form mixture into 4 equal patties, about 1/3 cup each and 3/4 to 1 inch thick. Place patties on a lined plate (with waxed paper, parchment or plastic wrap) and refrigerate for at least 30 minutes.

03. Spray or brush the air fryer basket with oil. Brush melted butter onto both sides of each crab cake and place in air fryer basket.

04. Cook at 350°F/176°C for 10 minutes, carefully flipping each crab cake halfway through.

05. Serve crab cakes with lemon wedges and a sauce, if desired.

PORK

Sausage, Potato, and Onion Bake

This sausage, potato, and onion recipe is a flavorful, easy, and filling dinner that is ready in less than 30 minutes!

PREP TIME: 7 minutes   **COOK TIME:** 22 minutes   **TOTAL TIME:** 29 minutes   **SERVES:** 4

RECIPE INGREDIENTS

- 1 1/2 lbs baby potatoes
- 2 bell peppers
- 1 sweet onion
- 12-14 oz precooked sausage
- 1-2 tsp avocado oil

INSTRUCTIONS

01. Preheat the air fryer to 400°F/200°C for 5 minutes.

02. Deseed pepper and cut into 1 inch pieces, peel and cut onion into quarters then separate layers, and wash and dry the potatoes (cut bigger potatoes in half).

03. Toss peppers and onions in bowl with 1-2 tsp of oil.

04. Place in air fryer basket. Add potatoes to air fryer basket and spray with oil.

05. Cook at 370°F/187°C for 10-12 minutes. Stir at halfway point.

06. While cooking, cut sausage into thick, bite-sized pieces (I did it in quarters).

07. Add sausage into the air fryer basket and cook for an additional 10 minutes. If you cut your sausage into smaller pieces, cook for about 3-5 minutes, or until potatoes are cooked through.

Sweet and Savory Ham with Honey Brown Sugar Glaze

Enjoy ham anytime of the year with this savory brown sugar honey glaze

PREP TIME: 5 minutes **COOK TIME:** 35 minutes **TOTAL TIME:** 40 minutes **SERVES:** 6

RECIPE INGREDIENTS

- 3-4 lb cooked ham pre-sliced

FOR GLAZE

- 1/2 c unsalted butter
- 1 c brown sugar
- 1/2 c honey
- 2 tbsp Dijon mustard
- 1/4 tsp cinnamon
- 1/4 tsp ground cloves
- 4 cloves garlic minced

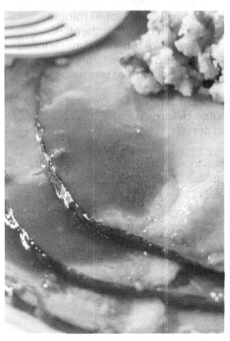

INSTRUCTIONS

01. Place 2 generous pieces of tinfoil in the air fryer.

02. Place pre-sliced ham in the middle of the tinfoil and tightly fold the tinfoil around the ham.

03. Heat the ham for 10 minutes at 350°F/176°C.

04. While the ham is warming, create the glaze. Brown the butter in a small saucepan over medium heat, until it begins to turn golden brown and aromatic. Swirl it around in the pan occasionally to help it brown evenly.

05. Stir in the brown sugar, honey, mustard, cinnamon, and cloves. Stir until sugar is dissolved, about 2 minutes.

06. Reduce heat to low and add the garlic. Cook for a minute or two until it becomes fragrant and just begins to simmer. Right as it begins to simmer, remove from heat and set aside. As it cools, it will become the consistency of a thick honey.

07. Open the tinfoil and brush or spoon 1/3 of the glaze over the ham. Refold the tinfoil and continue cooking for another 20 minutes at 350°F/176°C.

08. Open and fold down the tinfoil pushing it back from the meat. This will create a slightly crispy outer layer. Brush or spoon another 1/3 of the glaze over the ham and continue to cook at 350°F/176°C for another 5 minutes, checking occasionally to prevent burning edges.

09. The last 1/3 of the glaze can be used while serving the ham. It may need to be gently warmed for a few minutes again to thin out the glaze for serving since honey tends to thicken as it cools.

Pork Tenderloin with Balsamic Marinade

The air fryer is awesome for a lot of recipes, including this balsamic pork tenderloin. Cooked to tender, juicy perfection and so easy!

PREP TIME: 10 minutes   **COOK TIME:** 20 minutes   **TOTAL TIME:** 30 minutes   **SERVES:** 4

RECIPE INGREDIENTS

- ✓ 1 pork tenderloin, 1-1 1/2 lbs
- ✓ 3 tbsp balsamic vinegar
- ✓ 2 tbsp soy sauce
- ✓ 1 tsp lemon juice
- ✓ 2 tbsp brown sugar
- ✓ 1 1/2 tsp pepper
- ✓ 1 tsp kosher salt
- ✓ 1 tsp dried rosemary
- ✓ 1/2 tsp onion powder
- ✓ 1/2 tsp garlic powder

RECIPE NOTES

Don't confuse pork tenderloin with pork loin. Pork tenderloin is a long and narrow cut of meat. A pork loin will take much longer to cook and is not as tender.

INSTRUCTIONS

01. Remove excess fat and silver skin from tenderloin.

02. Add balsamic vinegar, soy sauce, lemon juice, brown sugar, pepper, kosher salt, rosemary, onion powder, and garlic powder to a gallon-size resealable plastic bag. Shake to mix. Add tenderloin to bag, roll up to keep marinade on pork, and seal. Let marinate refrigerated for at least 30 minutes, or as long as overnight.

03. Preheat air fryer to 400ºF/200ºC. Line air fryer with air fryer parchment paper or spray with cooking oil. Place tenderloin on parchment and cook at 400ºF/200ºC for 10 minutes. Flip tenderloin, then cook another 5-10 minutes, until internal temperature reaches 145ºF/63ºC. Cooking time will vary depending on your air fryer and size of tenderloin.

04. Remove tenderloin when done and let rest for 5 minutes before slicing. Cut into 1/2-inch slices and serve.

15 Minute Ranch Pork Chops

My new favorite way to cook pork chops.
It's so fast and easy! And they turn out perfectly every time.

PREP TIME: 5 minutes   **COOK TIME:** 10 minutes   **TOTAL TIME:** 15 minutes   **SERVES:** 4

RECIPE INGREDIENTS

- 4 boneless pork chops
- 2 tsp oil
- 1 tbsp ranch seasoning mix (see substitution on page 248)
- salt and pepper
- chopped parsley

INSTRUCTIONS

01 Pat pork chops dry with a paper towel. Drizzle the oil over both sides of each pork chop, spread to coat evenly. Sprinkle dry ranch seasoning mix evenly over both sides of each. Then season with salt and pepper.

02 Preheat air fryer to 380°F/193°C. Cook the pork chops for 10 minutes, flipping halfway, or until internal temperature of pork chops reaches 145°F/63°C. Cooking time may vary depending on thickness of the pork chops and your air fryer.

03 Garnish cooked pork chops with fresh chopped parsley, if desired.

Brown Sugar Pork Chops

This savory brown sugar rub on pork chops is our favorite go-to dinner on busy nights!

PREP TIME: 7 minutes   **COOK TIME:** 12 minutes   **TOTAL TIME:** 19 minutes   **SERVES:** 4

RECIPE INGREDIENTS

- 4 boneless pork chops, about 1" thick
- avocado or olive oil

RUB

- 2 tbsp brown sugar
- 1 tbsp paprika
- 2 tsp kosher salt
- 1 1/2 tsp ground black pepper
- 1 tsp ground mustard
- 1/2 tsp garlic powder

INSTRUCTIONS

01. Preheat the air fryer at 400°F/200°C for 5 minutes.

02. Mix the rub ingredients together.

03. Rinse and pat dry the pork chops.

04. Rub a little olive oil on each of the pork chops to help the rub adhere to it.

05. Liberally massage the rub into both sides of the pork chops.

06. Place the 2 pork chops in the air fryer basket (if your basket is bigger and can hold more, go for it).

07. Cook for 8-12 minutes at 400°F/200°C, turning at the halfway point.

08. Make sure the internal temperature of the pork chop registers at 145°F/63°C before enjoying.

VEGETABLES AND SIDES

Ratatouille Gnocchi

Whip up this tasty, healthy, and flavorful ratatouille gnocchi right in your air fryer. A perfect summer dish in under 30 minutes.

PREP TIME: 7 minutes   **COOK TIME:** 12 minutes   **TOTAL TIME:** 19 minutes   **SERVES:** 4

RECIPE INGREDIENTS

- 1 lb fresh gnocchi
- 4 cloves garlic minced
- 4 cups mixed vegetables zucchini, eggplants, tomatoes, bell pepper, red onion, all cut into bite sized pieces
- 1/4 c olive oil
- 2 tbsp balsamic vinegar
- salt and pepper, to taste
- 1/2-1 tbsp oil of choice

OPTIONAL

- 1 tsp maple syrup
- 2 tsp Herbes de Provence or Italian Seasoning

INSTRUCTIONS

01. In a large bowl, mix together the vegetables with olive oil, garlic, balsamic vinegar, salt, and pepper. Add maple syrup and herb de Provence if using.

02. In a separate bowl, mix the gnocchi together with 1/2 -1 tbsp of oil of choice. You just want to make the gnocchi covered in oil, but not too much. Season with salt and pepper.

03. Place the vegetables in the air fryer basket then add the gnocchi on top. Cook everything at 400°F/200°C for 15 minutes or until vegetables reach desired crispiness and gnocchi is heated through. Be sure to stir at the halfway point.

04. Remove from the air fryer basket and enjoy!

The Best Fried Rice

This air fryer fried rice recipe is easy, quick, and tasty!
Enjoy fried rice in less than 30 minutes thanks to the air fryer!

PREP TIME: 20 minutes   **COOK TIME:** 9 minutes   **TOTAL TIME:** 29 minutes   **SERVES:** 4

RECIPE INGREDIENTS

- 2-3 c cooked rice (day old rice is best)
- 1 c chicken cooked and chopped
- 1 c Asian frozen vegetables thawed
- 3 eggs scrambled
- 2 cloves garlic chopped
- 2 scallions sliced
- 2 tbsp soy sauce
- 1/2 tsp sesame oil

INSTRUCTIONS

01. Place the rice, vegetables, chicken, eggs, garlic, soy sauce, and sesame oil in an air fryer pan and stir together.

02. Cook at 380°F/193°C for 9 minutes. Stir well at the halfway point.

RECIPE NOTES

For additional flavor you can toss the chicken with teriyaki sauce, to your taste, and add 2 tsp of fried rice seasoning mix.

You can replicate the fried rice seasoning with 1 tsp ground ginger, 1/2 tsp salt, 1/4 tsp garlic powder, and 1 tsp sugar.

30 Minute Mac and Cheese

Creamy and cheesy – and ready in 30 minutes!

PREP TIME: 4 minutes   **COOK TIME:** 25 minutes   **TOTAL TIME:** 29 minutes   **SERVES:** 4

RECIPE INGREDIENTS

- ✓ 1 1/2 c raw elbow macaroni
- ✓ 1 1/4 c boiling or very hot water
- ✓ 2/3 c heavy cream
- ✓ 8 oz sharp cheddar cheese shredded and divided
- ✓ 1 tsp dry mustard (use 1/2 tsp of dry mustard if you aren't a fan of it)
- ✓ 1/2 tsp kosher salt or to taste
- ✓ 1/2 tsp black pepper
- ✓ 1/4 tsp garlic powder
- ✓ Optional: panko breadcrumbs and 1 tbsp melted butter

RECIPE NOTES

To quickly heat up the water, put it in your microwave for about 3 minutes. Cooking time will vary depending on your air fryer model. Keep an eye on your noodles and cheese, once they are cooked and melted to your liking it is finished.

INSTRUCTIONS

01. Combine uncooked elbow macaroni, HOT or BOILING water, and heavy cream, 2/3 of the cheese, dry mustard, kosher salt, black pepper, and garlic powder in a 7-inch pan oven proof pan that is deep enough to hold all the ingredients. Stir to combine.

02. Preheat the air fryer for 5 minutes at 400°F/200°C.

03. Place pan in air fryer basket, cover with tin foil tucking foil under pan, and cook for 20-25 minutes at 360°F/182°C. Every 10 minutes, carefully lift up foil and give the macaroni a quick stir. Tuck foil back under and continue cooking.

04. After 15 minutes, remove the foil, add the remaining cheese, and cook for 5 more minutes. Cook for an additional 3-5 minutes if needed.

Optional: After cooking for 20 minutes sprinkle panko crumbs over the top of the mac and cheese. Drizzle on 1 tbsp of melted butter. Cook for another 3-5 minutes until the top is golden.

Melting Roasted Potatoes

These roasted potatoes are an excellent side dish recipe!
And they are much faster than in the oven!

PREP TIME: 10 minutes   **COOK TIME:** 23 minutes   **TOTAL TIME:** 33 minutes   **SERVES:** 3

RECIPE INGREDIENTS

- ✔ 1 1/2 pounds potatoes peeled and cubed
- ✔ 2 tbsp butter melted
- ✔ 1/2 tsp dried thyme
- ✔ 1/3 tsp salt
- ✔ 1/8 tsp pepper
- ✔ 3/4 c chicken broth
- ✔ 1/2 tsp minced garlic

RECIPE NOTES

Cooking time may vary depending on your air fryer, the size of the potato pieces, and the type of potato. If your dish won't hold the potatoes comfortably, mix the potatoes, broth and garlic in a bowl and cook in two batches. Keep the first batch warm by transferring to a serving dish and tent with foil.

INSTRUCTIONS

01. Place peeled and cubed potatoes in a large bowl. Toss the potatoes with the melted butter, thyme, salt, and pepper, until evenly coated.

02. Add potatoes to air fryer and cook at 380°F/193°C for 12-15 minutes, tossing halfway through, edges should be browned.

03. Transfer the potatoes to an oven-safe shallow dish that will fit in your air fryer. Spread potatoes to be in as much of a single layer as possible. Pour broth into dish and add minced garlic; stir to coat.

04. Cook a 380°F/193°C for 8 more minutes. Carefully remove dish and let sit for a few minutes. Serve warm, pouring any remaining sauce from the pan over the potatoes, and enjoy!

Easy Roasted Potatoes

One of my favorite side dish recipes - air fryer roasted potatoes are easy and delicious!

PREP TIME: 10 minutes   **COOK TIME:** 12 minutes   **TOTAL TIME:** 22 minutes   **SERVES:** 4

RECIPE INGREDIENTS

- 1 lb Yukon gold potatoes
- 1 tbsp olive oil or avocado oil
- 1/2 tsp garlic powder
- 1/2 tsp onion powder
- 1/4 tsp paprika
- 1/2 tsp salt

RECIPE NOTES

Leftovers can be reheated in air fryer at 350°F/176°C for about 5-10 minutes.

INSTRUCTIONS

01. Preheat air fryer to 380°F/193°C. Cut potatoes into 1- or 2-inch chunks, keeping them about the same size for more even cooking.

02. In a large bowl, toss the potatoes with the oil, garlic powder, onion powder, paprika, and salt.

03. Transfer seasoned potatoes to air fryer in a single layer. Cook at 380°F/193°C for 12-15 minutes, until browned and crispy on the outside and tender on the inside. Serve warm.

Baked Potatoes

Get perfect baked potatoes that are crispy on the outside and fluffy on the inside - all in less time - with this simple air fryer recipe.

PREP TIME: 5 minutes   **COOK TIME:** 40 minutes   **TOTAL TIME:** 45 minutes   **SERVES:** 4

RECIPE INGREDIENTS

- 4 medium russet potatoes washed, unpeeled
- 1/2 tsp avocado oil
- salt and pepper

RECIPE NOTES

Lightly oiling and salting the outside of the potatoes gives them awesome, crisp, well-seasoned skins.

Try some new flavors by adding something like garlic salt, garlic powder, rosemary, and/or parsley on the outside of the potatoes.

INSTRUCTIONS

01 Lightly prick each potato several times with a fork. Make sure potatoes are dry first, then rub them with oil and sprinkle with salt.

02 Arrange potatoes in the air fryer basket, with space between them.

03 Cook at 400°F/200°C for 40-45 minutes, until a knife can be inserted with little resistance.

Transfer potatoes to a plate, use a knife to cut two slits, forming an X, in each potato. Press in at ends of each potato to push the inside up and out. Season with salt and pepper, to taste.

04 Serve with your favorite toppings!

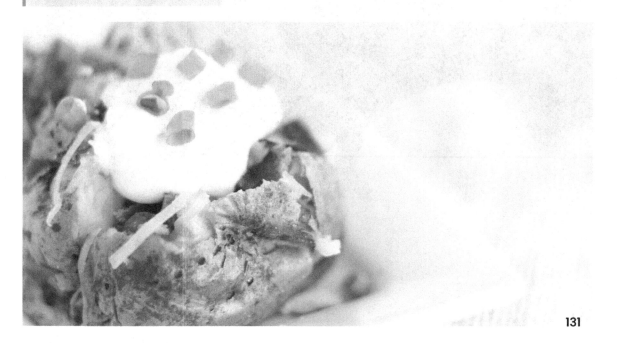

132

Hasselback Potatoes

Hasselback potatoes take half the time in the air fryer
than cooking them in the oven and tastes so good too!

PREP TIME: 10 minutes   **COOK TIME:** 25 minutes   **TOTAL TIME:** 35 minutes   **SERVES:** 5

RECIPE INGREDIENTS

FOR THE POTATOES

- 5 medium russet or other baking potatoes
- olive oil
- flake salt
- Tony's Cajun seasoning

FOR THE TOPPINGS

- 2 slices of bacon, chopped
- chives, chopped
- parmesan cheese
- sour cream
- ranch dressing mix

INSTRUCTIONS

01. Wash and dry the potatoes.

02. Place chopsticks, table knives or hard plastic straws on either long side of a potato. Thinly slice the potatoes being careful to not cut all the way through. The chopsticks provide an even depth.

03. Oil the potatoes, spreading the slices gently and sprinkle on the salt and Cajun seasoning to taste.

04. Preheat the air fryer at 400°F/200°C for 5 minutes.

05. Place the potatoes in the air fryer without crowding and cook at 350°F/176°C for 15-20 minutes. Check in on the potatoes at 15 minutes, if they aren't cooked through, cook for an extra 5-6 minutes until tender inside but crispy on the outside.

06. While the potatoes are baking, prepare your toppings.

07. For ranch sour cream, mix together ranch and sour cream.

08. Once your potatoes are cooked, top with your favorite toppings and enjoy!

Homemade French Fries

Learn how to make perfect, crispy air fryer French fries at home! They're healthier than regular oven-baked or fast food fries so you can eat them guilt-free.

PREP TIME: 20 minutes   **COOK TIME:** 30 minutes   **TOTAL TIME:** 50 minutes   **SERVES:** 4

RECIPE INGREDIENTS

- ✓ 1 1/2 pounds russet potatoes washed and dried
- ✓ 2 tbsp avocado oil divided
- ✓ 1/2 tsp salt
- ✓ 1/4 tsp garlic powder
- ✓ salt and pepper to taste

INSTRUCTIONS

01 Cut potatoes lengthwise into 1/2-inch thick slices or planks, then slice the planks into 1/2-inch thick sticks for the fries.

02 Place the potatoes in a medium or large bowl and add enough water to cover them. Drain and repeat until the water stays clear.

03 Cover potatoes with hot tap water and let sit for 10 minutes. Drain water and pat potatoes dry with a clean lint-free towel or paper towel.

04 In a dry bowl, gently toss potatoes with 1 tbsp oil. Transfer potatoes to air fryer basket. Set bowl aside for later. Cook at 350°F/176°C for 8 minutes.

05 Dump potatoes into bowl and gently toss to redistribute. Return potatoes to air fryer and cook until softened and potatoes have turned from white to blond, 5-10 minutes.

06 Transfer potatoes back to bowl and gently toss with remaining 1 tbsp oil, 1/2 tsp salt, and 1/4 tsp garlic powder. Return to air fryer and cook at 400°F/200°C, until golden brown and crisp, 15-20 minutes, tossing gently every 5 minutes to redistribute (it may be easier to quickly toss in the bowl than the basket).

07 Transfer fries to a plate and season with salt and pepper to taste. Serve immediately.

Homemade Tater Tots

You will love these fluffy, charming and simple tater tots in the air fryer.
You can even serve it as an after school snack for the kids (or yourself!)

PREP TIME: 30 minutes   **COOK TIME:** 14 minutes   **TOTAL TIME:** 44 minutes   **SERVES:** 2

RECIPE INGREDIENTS

- ✓ 3 medium russet potatoes
- ✓ salt to taste
- ✓ pepper to taste
- ✓ seasoning of choice to taste
- ✓ avocado oil spray

INSTRUCTIONS

01 Scrub potatoes, and cut into quarters.

02 Boil for 5 minutes, let cool for 10 minutes.

03 Grate boiled potatoes, including as much potato skin as desired.

04 Mix in salt, pepper, or seasonings of choice. (These tater tots are full of potato flavor and really don't need much seasoning. You could omit the seasonings and/or salt, if desired).

05 Spray bottom of air fryer with avocado oil.

06 Spray hands with avocado oil and quickly roll about 2 tbsp of potato mixture between your hands into small ovals - they will be sticky.

07 Place tater tots into air fryer spaced 1/2 inch apart.

08 Lightly spray the tater tots again.

09 Bake at 370°F/187°C for 14 minutes or until golden brown, flipping halfway through.

10 Remove from the air fryer basket and enjoy!

Easy Baked Sweet Potatoes

All you need is a little salt and oil to enjoy these deliciously baked sweet potatoes as a snack, side, or treat!

PREP TIME: 5 minutes   **COOK TIME:** 40 minutes   **TOTAL TIME:** 45 minutes   **SERVES:** 2

RECIPE INGREDIENTS

- ✔ 2 sweet potatoes
- ✔ Kosher salt to taste
- ✔ avocado oil or oil of your choice

RECIPE NOTES

The cooking time will depend greatly on the size of your potatoes. So just keep an eye on your potatoes, and pull them out when a thin knife or fork goes in easily. If you are cooking sweet potatoes for multiple people, remember to not overcrowd your basket. Leave room for air to flow, so that your sweet potatoes can bake.

INSTRUCTIONS

01. Wash and scrub your sweet potatoes so they are clean and free from dirt.

02. Pierce your potatoes with a fork, 4-5 times.

03. Place potatoes in the air fryer basket and spray with oil. Rub oil all over the sweet potatoes.

04. Sprinkle with Kosher salt.

05. Bake sweet potatoes at 380°F/193°C for 40 minutes. At the halfway point, carefully flip potatoes over.

06. After they finish cooking, give your sweet potatoes a squeeze. If your potatoes need more time, add a couple of minutes until they are cooked to desired tenderness. The cooking time really depends on the size of your potatoes, so you will just have to watch it carefully.

Sweet Potato Fries

Say goodbye to processed sweet potato fries!
These are delicious and healthy!

PREP TIME: 10 minutes   **COOK TIME:** 15 minutes   **TOTAL TIME:** 25 minutes   **SERVES:** 1-2

RECIPE INGREDIENTS

- 1-2 small sweet potatoes
- 1 tsp salt
- 2 tsp avocado oil
- 1 tsp onion powder
- 1 tsp garlic powder
- 1-1 1/2 tsp paprika
- 1/4-1/2 tsp oregano
- Chili powder, to taste

INSTRUCTIONS

01 Preheat the air fryer for 5 minutes at 400°F/200°C.

02 Peel the potatoes and cut them into 1/4-1/2 inch thick slices. Place them in a bowl of cold water and let it soak for about 5 minutes.

03 Drain the potatoes from the water and pat them completely dry. Dry out the bowl. Make sure the fries are completely dry. Place the fries back in the bowl, add the salt.

04 Add the oil to the fries with the seasonings. You can add more or less of the seasoning, it is completely to your taste. I recommend having more of the garlic, onion, and paprika over the oregano and chili powder. But feel free to experiment with your own favorite seasonings. Stir to combine the seasonings with the oil and potatoes.

05 Place the fries in a single layer in the air fryer basket. Cook at 370°F/187°C for 12-15 minutes or until the fries reach desired tenderness, shaking at the halfway point.

06 Once the fries are tender to your liking, bump up the heat to 400°F/200°C and cook for 2-3 minutes or until they reach desired crispiness.

07 Enjoy with your favorite dipping sauce! (I made a combination of mayonnaise and BBQ sauce).

Sweet Potato Casserole

An incredibly delicious side that could almost be considered dessert!

PREP TIME: 20 minutes   **COOK TIME:** 10 minutes   **TOTAL TIME:** 30 minutes   **SERVES:** 6

RECIPE INGREDIENTS

- 2 lbs sweet potato, peeled and cubed
- 1/2 c white sugar
- 2 eggs beaten
- 1/2 tsp salt
- 4 tbsp butter softened
- 1/2 c milk
- 1/2 tsp vanilla extract

TOPPINGS

- 2 c miniature marshmallows
- 1/3 c brown sugar packed
- 1/4 c all-purpose flour
- 3 tbsp butter softened
- 1/2 c chopped pecans optional

INSTRUCTIONS

01. Add cut sweet potatoes and 1 cup water into the Instant Pot. Make sure that the release valve is in the "Sealing" position. Place the lid on, turn and lock.

02. Press the "Manual" button on the Instant Pot on high pressure, and then set the timer to 10 minutes. When the potatoes finish, quickly release the pressure and drain the water.

03. If you do not have an Instant Pot, boil the potatoes until they are fork tender.

04. Place the potatoes in a bowl and add sugar, eggs, salt, butter, milk and vanilla.

05. Mix until smooth.

06. Transfer to an 8x8 baking dish, 7" cake barrel air fryer accessory, or five 8 oz ramekins.

07. In a small bowl mix together the brown sugar and flour. Cut in the softened butter to make a fine crumble. Pour on top of the sweet potatoes in an even layer and lightly press down.

08. Place in the air fryer and cook for 6 minutes at 320°F/160°C or until mixture is heated through. Add the marshmallows and chopped pecans to the top, press down lightly, and cook for an additional 3-4 minutes.

Blooming Onion

*Make a tastier and healthier blooming onion in the air fryer with
a creamy dipping sauce that everyone will love!*

PREP TIME: 25 minutes   **COOK TIME:** 20 minutes   **TOTAL TIME:** 45 minutes   **SERVES:** 12

RECIPE INGREDIENTS

- ✓ 1 large sweet onion

ONION BREADING

- ✓ 1-1 1/2 c flour, depending on the size of your onion
- ✓ 1 tbsp paprika
- ✓ 1 tbsp brown sugar
- ✓ 1 tsp salt
- ✓ 1/2 tsp cayenne pepper
- ✓ 1/2 tsp pepper
- ✓ 1/2 tsp dried oregano
- ✓ 1/2 tsp dried thyme
- ✓ 1/2 tsp ground cumin
- ✓ 1 c panko breadcrumbs

LIQUID DREDGE

- ✓ 2 eggs
- ✓ 3/4-1 c buttermilk (see substitution on page 248)

DIPPING SAUCE

- ✓ 2 tbsp sour cream
- ✓ 2 tbsp mayonnaise
- ✓ 1 tbsp creamy horseradish
- ✓ 2 tsp ketchup
- ✓ 1/2 tsp Sriracha sauce

INSTRUCTIONS

01. Cut off the top portion of the onion and peel off the outer skin.

02. Flip the onion over and trim off the roots, if needed.

03. With the bottom side down, cut straight through from top to bottom working around the center of the onion and being sure not to cut all the way through. You should end with approximately 16-20 sections.

04. Soak onion in ice water while you make up the mixtures.

05. Mix all dry ingredients together in a medium bowl.

06. In another medium bowl combine the eggs and milk until smooth. Add 1/4 cup of the flour mixture to the milk mixture and whisk until smooth.

07. On a large plate, place 1 cup panko crumbs and lightly spray with oil of your choice.

08. Remove onion from the ice water and let it drain cut-side down for a minute.

09. Working with the cut side up, coat the onion in the flour mixture making sure to get flour in between onion petals.

10. Then soak the onion in the milk mixture, again opening petals to ensure milk gets into the flour mixture.

- 1/2 tsp Worcestershire sauce
- 1/2 tsp salt
- 1/4 tsp paprika

11. Then place onion back into flour bowl, cut side up, and pour panko crumb mixture over the top of the onion, working to get crumbs between each onion petal.

12. Make a foil sling by folding some foil into a somewhat long narrow strip and making two handles at the end of the foil that will hang over the side of the basket.

13. Place foil sling into the air fryer basket with excess foil hanging evenly over sides, Place onion on top of the foil and spray with oil.

14. Cover with foil, securing the two long side 'handles' under the onion and leaving the other two sides open for air flow.

15. Cook at 370°F/187°C for 15 minutes. Fold back the long foil and then cook for 3-5 minutes more, depending on the size of your onion and your air fryer wattage. The final result should be nice and toasty with just some light charring on the ends of your onion.

16. Using the excess foil handles, lift the onion onto your serving platter and enjoy with dipping sauce.

17. Mix all ingredients for the dipping sauce.

18. Refrigerate until ready to enjoy.

Green Beans

Fresh green beans are a delight in the air fryer! Cook as little or as long as you like, to achieve your favorite level of tenderness.

PREP TIME: 5 minutes   **COOK TIME:** 15 minutes   **TOTAL TIME:** 20 minutes   **SERVES:** 4

RECIPE INGREDIENTS

- Fresh Green beans

INSTRUCTIONS

01 Wash the green beans and chop off the ends.

02 Dry the green beans in the air fryer basket for about 5 minutes at 350°F/175°C.

03 Spray with avocado oil and toss the green beans in the air fryer basket.

04 Add salt and pepper and cook for 5-10 minutes more at 350°F/175°C.

Roasted Sweet Potatoes

Another simple way to enjoy sweet potatoes!

PREP TIME: 20 minutes   **COOK TIME:** 6 minutes   **TOTAL TIME:** 26 minutes   **SERVES:** 16

RECIPE INGREDIENTS

- 1-2 lbs sweet potatoes
- 1-2 tbsp oil
- sea salt, to taste

INSTRUCTIONS

01 Peel and chop the sweet potatoes into 1/2 inch cubes.

02 Toss with your choice of healthy oil and sea salt.

03 Place in the air fryer basket and cook for 10-12 minutes at 360°F/182°C or until the sweet potatoes reach desired tenderness.

Sautéed Onions

*Tasty and easy sautéed onions cook up in a flash in the air fryer!
Whip them up to add to sandwiches, burgers, or salads!*

PREP TIME: 5 minutes   **COOK TIME:** 10 minutes   **TOTAL TIME:** 15 minutes   **SERVES:** 4

RECIPE INGREDIENTS

- 1 large onion
- avocado oil
- salt to taste

INSTRUCTIONS

01 Cut the onion into slices and separate into rings.

02 Spray the air fryer basket and place the onions inside.

03 Lightly spray the onions with oil and sprinkle on salt.

04 Cook in the air fryer for 380°F/193°C for 10 minutes, stirring at the halfway point.

Sweet Roasted Butternut Squash

If you love roasted butternut squash, you'll love making it in the air fryer!
It's ready in HALF the time!

PREP TIME: 5 minutes   **COOK TIME:** 27 minutes   **TOTAL TIME:** 32 minutes   **SERVES:** 4

RECIPE INGREDIENTS

- ✓ 1 medium butternut squash
- ✓ 1 tbsp butter melted
- ✓ 2 tbsp brown sugar
- ✓ 1/4 tsp cinnamon

RECIPE NOTES

This will also work with acorn squash. Air fry at 370°F/187°C for 20-25 minutes or until squash reaches desired tenderness.

INSTRUCTIONS

01 Wash outside of squash, cut off the stem end, and cut squash in half lengthwise. Use a spoon to scrape out and discard the seeds and stringy flesh. Use a knife to score the flesh of the squash, crisscross.

02 Pour the melted butter evenly over both halves of the squash. Then sprinkle each half of the squash with 1 tbsp of brown sugar and sprinkle cinnamon over top. For a less sweet version, use a total of 1/2 tbsp brown sugar and lightly season with pepper and kosher salt instead.

03 Place prepared squash in a single layer in air fryer basket, flesh-side up. Cook at 380°F/193°C for 27 minutes, or until tender.

Roasted Asparagus

This is my go-to way to cook asparagus now. I love how easy, quick and delicious it is.

PREP TIME: 5 minutes   **COOK TIME:** 6 minutes   **TOTAL TIME:** 11 minutes   **SERVES:** 4

RECIPE INGREDIENTS

- ✔ 1 lb asparagus
- ✔ 1 tsp olive oil or avocado oil
- ✔ 1/8 tsp salt
- ✔ 1/8 tsp pepper
- ✔ lemon wedges

INSTRUCTIONS

01 Rinse asparagus and dry well. Holding the center and bottom of each spear, snap off the bottom and discard.

02 Toss asparagus with oil, salt, and pepper in a bowl or pan. Transfer to air fryer basket.

03 Cook at 400°F/200°C until tender and bright green, 6 to 8 minutes, tossing half way through.

04 Season with additional salt and pepper, if desired. Serve with lemon wedges. (For a brighter flavor, top with gremolata.)

Corn on the Cob

10 minutes is all you need for perfect corn on the cob!

PREP TIME: 2 minutes   **COOK TIME:** 10 minutes   **TOTAL TIME:** 12 minutes   **SERVES:** 4

RECIPE INGREDIENTS

- 4 ears of corn, husked and trimmed
- avocado oil
- salt and pepper, to taste

INSTRUCTIONS

01 Spray or rub oil all over the prepared ears of corn. Place corn in the air fryer. If the ears of corn do not fit in your air fryer, breaking the ears of corn in half might help.

02 Cook for 8-10 minutes at 400°F/200°C, flipping ears halfway through cook time.

03 Serve with butter and salt and pepper. Enjoy!

Brussels Sprouts with Bacon & Maple Syrup

Make these easy and delicious maple bacon Brussels sprouts in less than 30 minutes for an easy dinner or side dish.

PREP TIME: 10 minutes   **COOK TIME:** 15 minutes   **TOTAL TIME:** 25 minutes   **SERVES:** 4

RECIPE INGREDIENTS

- 1 pound Brussels sprouts
- 1/4 c avocado oil
- 1/4 c pure maple syrup
- 1 tbsp apple cider vinegar
- 1/2 tsp salt
- 1/4 tsp pepper
- 4 bacon slices, cut into 1/2-inch pieces

INSTRUCTIONS

01 Trim and halve the washed Brussels sprouts, removing discolored leaves. Larger sprouts may need to be quartered to keep sprouts uniform in size.

02 In a medium bowl, whisk together oil, maple syrup, vinegar, salt, and pepper.

03 Add Brussels sprouts and raw bacon pieces to the bowl and gently stir to coat.

04 Spoon coated sprouts and bacon into the air fryer. (Note that any extra glaze/sauce will just fall to the bottom of the air fryer.)

05 Cook at 350°F/176°C for 10-15 minutes, until bacon and sprouts reach desired crispiness. Halfway through cooking, open drawer and stir contents.

Fall Roasted Brussels Sprouts

Paired with apples, pecans, and dried cranberries,
this roasted Brussels sprouts salad will be a hit at your next meal.

PREP TIME: 10 minutes   **COOK TIME:** 15 minutes   **TOTAL TIME:** 25 minutes   **SERVES:** 4

RECIPE INGREDIENTS

- 1 lb Brussels sprouts, trimmed and halved
- 2 tbsp avocado oil
- 1/4 tsp kosher salt
- 1/4 tsp freshly ground pepper
- 1/2 tsp cayenne seasoning
- 1 cup sliced apples (I used Honeycrisp)
- 1/2 cup dried cranberries
- 1/4 cup chopped pecans
- 1/4 cup red wine vinaigrette

INSTRUCTIONS

01 Preheat the air fryer to 350°F/176°C for 5 minutes.

02 In a bowl, mix together to evenly coat the Brussels sprouts with olive oil, salt, pepper, and cayenne pepper.

03 Place the prepared Brussels sprouts in the air fryer basket and cook for 10-15 minutes. Halfway through cooking, open and mix in the sliced apple, dried cranberries, and chopped pecans. Continue roasting for another 10-15 minutes or until sprouts and apples reach desired crispiness.

04 Remove from the air fryer basket and transfer to a serving platter. Drizzle with red wine vinaigrette. Serve immediately.

Savory Carrots

Enjoy roasted carrots in half the time with this easy recipe!

PREP TIME: 5 minutes   **COOK TIME:** 15 minutes   **TOTAL TIME:** 20 minutes   **SERVES:** 2

RECIPE INGREDIENTS

- 4 large carrots
- 1 tbsp olive oil
- 1/4 tsp salt
- 1/4 tsp pepper
- 1 tsp Italian seasoning

INSTRUCTIONS

01 Prepare the carrots by peeling and cutting into French fry-sized strips.

02 In a large bowl, drizzle the olive oil and seasonings over the carrots and toss well.

03 Place in an even layer in the air fryer basket and cook at 350°F/176°C for 5 minutes. Stir the carrots gently then continue cooking for an additional 10-15 minutes or until the carrots reach the desired tenderness.

04 Sprinkle additional seasonings if desired and serve with a side of ranch dressing.

Buffalo Cauliflower Bites

*These easy buffalo cauliflower bites are Keto-friendly,
healthy, flavorful, and so simple to make.*

PREP TIME: 6 minutes   **COOK TIME:** 15 minutes   **TOTAL TIME:** 21 minutes   **SERVES:** 6

RECIPE INGREDIENTS

- 1 head cauliflower cut into small bites
- cooking oil
- 1/2 c buffalo wing sauce
- 1 tbsp butter melted
- salt and pepper to taste

RECIPE NOTES

If you find the cauliflower is not crisping, spritz with a bit more oil. The longer you cook the cauliflower, the more it will crisp.

INSTRUCTIONS

01 Spray the air fryer basket with cooking oil.

02 Add the cauliflower bites to the air fryer. Spray with cooking oil. Cook for 7 minutes at 400°F/200°C.

03 Place the melted butter, buffalo sauce, salt and pepper to taste in a bowl. Stir until well combined and set aside.

04 Open the air fryer and transfer the cauliflower in a large mixing bowl. Drizzle the butter mixture over top and stir until everything is evenly coated.

05 Return the cauliflower back to the air fryer. Cook at 400°F/200°C for 7-8 minutes until the cauliflower bites are crisp. (Every air fryer brand is different. Be sure to use your personal judgment to assist with optimal cook time).

06 Remove the cauliflower from the air fryer and serve.

Roasted Fall Vegetables

Flavorful, tasty, and easy, this recipe is not only perfect for the fall, but also for busy nights and picky eaters!

PREP TIME: 6 minutes   **COOK TIME:** 15 minutes   **TOTAL TIME:** 21 minutes   **SERVES:** 6

RECIPE INGREDIENTS

- 1 sweet potato peeled and cubed
- 1/2 lb butternut squash peeled and cubed
- 10 baby potatoes sliced in half
- 3 carrots peeled and halved
- 8 oz baby bella, (cremini), mushrooms
- 1 red onion cut into wedges
- 1 head of garlic peeled
- 2 tbsp extra virgin olive oil or avocado oil
- 2 tbsp balsamic vinegar
- 1 1/2 tbsp Italian seasoning
- fresh thyme to taste
- 2 tsp salt or to taste
- freshly cracked pepper to taste

INSTRUCTIONS

01. Preheat the air fryer at 400°F/200°C for 5 minutes.

02. Keep the potatoes, sweet potatoes, and squash separate from the rest of the veggies, but toss everything in the oil and spices.

03. Start with the sweet potatoes, potatoes, and squash in the air fryer basket and cook for 350°F/176°C for 12 minutes.

04. Add remaining veggies and cook for 10-14 more minutes at 350°F/176°C or until tender and crispy.

Korean Fried Cauliflower

If you've never had air-fried cauliflower, this Korean fried cauliflower is a great recipe to start with. It's full of flavor, healthy, and makes for a great snack too!

PREP TIME: 20 minutes   **COOK TIME:** 40 minutes   **TOTAL TIME:** 60 minutes   **SERVES:** 4

RECIPE INGREDIENTS

- 1 head cauliflower cut into bite-size florets (about 1 1/2 pounds florets)
- 1 tbsp cornstarch
- pinch salt
- pinch pepper
- pinch baking powder

BATTER

- 1 c all-purpose flour
- 1/2 c cornstarch
- 2 tsp baking powder
- 1 tbsp garlic powder
- 1 c cold water

SAUCE

- 4 1/2 tbsp gochujang Korean chili sauce
- 4 tbsp reduced sodium soy sauce
- 3 tbsp honey
- 1 tsp sesame oil
- 1/2 tsp freshly grated ginger
- 1/2 tsp minced garlic

INSTRUCTIONS

01. In a small bowl, mix together 1 tbsp cornstarch with a pinch each of salt, pepper, and baking powder. Sprinkle cauliflower florets with the mixture and stir to coat.

02. In a large bowl, whisk together the flour, cornstarch, baking powder, and garlic powder for the batter. Then add the cold water. The batter will be on the thick side, kind of like pancake batter.

03. Dip the cauliflower into the batter to coat, shake a little over the bowl to allow excess batter to drip off, then place the coated cauliflower on a wire rack (with a paper towel underneath) to allow more excess batter to drip off. Better for excess to drip off before it goes into the air fryer.

04. Brush the air fryer basket with a light layer of oil to help reduce sticking. Place coated cauliflower into the air fryer basket in a single layer, with space between each floret. Cook at 350°F/176°C for 10-12 minutes, until parts are light golden brown. (For my air fryer, this took 4 batches to cook all cauliflower. Remove debris and recoat basket with oil between each batch).

05. While the cauliflower is cooking, you can finish dipping the remaining cauliflower florets, then work on the sauce. Whisk together the gochujang, soy sauce, honey, sesame oil, ginger, garlic, and vinegar in a small saucepan. Bring to a simmer over medium heat, then remove from heat.

- ✅ 1/4 tsp rice vinegar or apple cider vinegar

- ✅ **Garnishes:** lime zest sesame seeds, green onions, lime wedges, and/or Ranch dressing

06 Once cauliflower is done cooking, add it to a large bowl. Then pour the sauce over the cauliflower and gently stir to coat.

07 Serve immediately. If desired, garnish with lime zest, lime wedges, green onion, and sesame seeds. Delicious served with a side of Ranch dressing.

RECIPE NOTES

Sauce can be mixed together up to 3 days in advance. Cover and refrigerate it, then bring to a simmer right before serving.

Cook time may vary and will depend on how many batches it takes for you to air fry the cauliflower florets.

Zucchini Fries

Got zucchini? Try these zucchini fries in the air fryer!
Easy, fast, healthy, and delicious!

PREP TIME: 5 minutes   **COOK TIME:** 10 minutes   **TOTAL TIME:** 15 minutes   **SERVES:** 4

RECIPE INGREDIENTS

- ✓ 1 medium zucchini about 10 oz
- ✓ 1 large egg
- ✓ 1/2 c panko or almond flour or bread crumbs
- ✓ 1/2 c grated Parmesan
- ✓ 3/4 tsp Italian seasoning
- ✓ 1/4 tsp garlic powder
- ✓ pinch of salt and pepper
- ✓ oil for spraying

OPTIONAL YOGURT DIP

- ✓ 1/2 c plain yogurt
- ✓ 1/2 tsp lemon zest
- ✓ 1 tbsp fresh lemon juice
- ✓ 1/4 tsp salt
- ✓ 1/8 tsp pepper

INSTRUCTIONS

01. Cut the zucchini in half lengthwise, then cut each of those pieces in half lengthwise again. Using a vegetable peeler, shave seeds from inner portion of each zucchini quarter. Then cut the pieces in half crosswise, so you end up with 16 pieces total that are about 1/2-inch thick and 3 to 4 inches long.

02. In a shallow bowl, lightly beat the egg. In another shallow bowl, combine the panko (or almond flour or breadcrumbs), parmesan, Italian seasoning, garlic powder, salt and pepper.

03. Dredge the zucchini pieces in the egg, then in the crumb mixture. Gently press crumbs to zucchini to coat and adhere.

04. Lightly spray the air fryer basket with oil. Arrange half of the zucchini pieces in the basket in a single layer, spaced evenly apart. Spray zucchini with oil to help evenly brown. Arrange remaining zucchini on top, perpendicular to first layer. Spray with oil.

05. Cook at 400°F/200°C for 9-10 minutes, or until breading is crisp and golden.

06. For the yogurt dip, whisk the yogurt, lemon zest, juice, salt and pepper together in a small bowl.

Zucchini Corn Fritters

These fritters make an excellent side dish or can be enjoyed as a healthy and tasty snack.

PREP TIME: 15 minutes   **COOK TIME:** 15 minutes   **TOTAL TIME:** 30 minutes   **SERVES:** 4

RECIPE INGREDIENTS

- 2 medium zucchini grated
- 1 c corn kernels fresh or frozen
- 1 medium potato cooked, peeled, mashed
- 4 tbsp flour of your choice
- 2-3 garlic finely minced
- 2-3 tsp olive oil
- salt and pepper

INSTRUCTIONS

01 In strainer mix grated zucchini with a little salt and leave it for 10-15 minutes. Then squeeze out excess water from the zucchini using clean hands or a cheesecloth.

02 Cook the potato in a microwave for 3-4 minutes or until tender. Then place in cold water for a few minutes. Peel and then grate or mash.

03 Combine zucchini, potato, corn, flour, garlic, salt, and pepper in a mixing bowl.

04 Roughly take 2 tbsp batter, give it a shape of a patty (about the size of your palm) and place it on parchment or wax paper lined plate or baking sheet. Lightly brush oil on the surface of each fritter. Preheat the air fryer to 360°F/182°C for 4 minutes.

05 Place the fritters in the preheated air fryer and arrange so that they are not touching each other. Cook them for 9 minutes.

06 Then turn the fritters and cook for another 4-5 minutes or until well done or till you get the desired color and crunchiness.

07 Serve warm with dipping sauce of your choice.

RECIPE NOTES

The purpose of the flour is to soak up some of the moisture from the ingredients. If you use minced garlic from a jar, soak up some of the oil by placing the minced garlic on a paper towel first so you don't add any more moisture.

Zucchini Tomato Corn Salad

This amazing corn salad is wonderful topped over spinach!
Enjoy the optional homemade dressing recipe, or use your own favorite vinaigrette.

PREP TIME: 8 minutes   **COOK TIME:** 9 minutes   **TOTAL TIME:** 17 minutes   **SERVES:** 4

RECIPE INGREDIENTS

- 2 c chopped zucchini
- 2 c cherry tomatoes
- 2 c frozen corn kernels
- salt and pepper, to taste
- spinach, for serving
- feta cheese, for serving

HOMEMADE DRESSING (OPTIONAL)

- 1/4 c red wine vinegar
- 2 tbsp fresh lemon juice
- 1 tsp honey
- 1/3 c olive oil

INSTRUCTIONS

01 Preheat the air fryer at 400°F/200°C for 5 minutes.

02 Spray the air fryer basket and pour in the zucchini & tomatoes. Lightly spray the tops of the vegetables and season with salt and pepper. Cook at 400°F/200°C for 5-6 minutes.

03 Stir in the corn and cook for an additional 2-3 minutes or until veggies reach desired tenderness and crispiness.

04 Make the salad dressing by combining the red wine vinegar, lemon juice, honey, and olive oil.

05 Remove from the air fryer basket and serve on top of spinach, or other leafy green of your choice. Top the salad with dressing and feta cheese.

NOTES

SNACKS AND SANDWICHES

Pepperoni Stromboli

I love how quick and easy Stromboli is in the air fryer!
An easy meal that the whole family loves.

PREP TIME: 15 minutes   **COOK TIME:** 10 minutes   **TOTAL TIME:** 25 minutes   **SERVES:** 6

RECIPE INGREDIENTS

- ✅ 1 3/4 c self rising flour
- ✅ 1 c non-fat plain Greek yogurt
- ✅ 4 tbsp pizza sauce plus extra for dipping
- ✅ 1 c shredded mozzarella cheese plus extra for topping
- ✅ 2 1/2 oz pepperoni
- ✅ 1 egg beaten

RECIPE NOTES

Any pizza dough, homemade or store bought, will work for this recipe.

INSTRUCTIONS

01. In a large mixing bowl or stand mixer, combine self rising flour and Greek yogurt until a thick dough forms. Dough will be shaggy and thick, but should mostly stick together when pressed into a ball. Roll out dough into a 10"x14" rectangle on a lightly floured surface. Cut the rectangle of dough in half to form two rectangles (to fit in the air fryer).

02. Spread about 2 tbsp pizza sauce on each rectangle, leaving a 2-inch border around the edges. Sprinkle 1/2 cup cheese over the sauce on each, then top with pepperoni.

03. Roll the rectangles of dough up into logs, like you would with cinnamon rolls. Pinch the edges together and tuck and pinch the ends under. Brush the tops of the stromboli with the beaten egg. Sprinkle additional cheese over top. Use a sharp knife to gently cut diagonal slit, every 2 inches, on the top of each stromboli.

04. Preheat air fryer for 5 minutes. Spray air fryer basket lightly with oil. Place both Stromboli in the air fryer basket, if they will fit without touching each other. Cook at 340°F/170°C for about 10 minutes, until golden brown and cooked through. Let rest for a few minutes, then cut into slices and serve with extra pizza sauce for dipping.

Roast Beef Stromboli

Roast beef Stromboli is a fun and tasty variation of pepperoni Stromboli.
Ready in minutes, this recipe will be a quick family favorite.

PREP TIME: 10 minutes   **COOK TIME:** 17 minutes   **TOTAL TIME:** 27 minutes   **SERVES:** 4

RECIPE INGREDIENTS

- ✓ 1 pizza crust (I used a thin crust, but you can use whatever type of crust you love)
- ✓ 1/2 red or yellow onion, sliced
- ✓ 6 oz sliced mushrooms (8-10 mushrooms)
- ✓ 1 bell pepper, sliced
- ✓ 12-16 slices of roast beef
- ✓ olive oil
- ✓ 6-8 provolone slices
- ✓ shredded provolone cheese - optional
- ✓ 1 egg wash

PROVOLONE CHEESE SAUCE (OPTIONAL)

- ✓ 2 tbsp butter
- ✓ 3 tbsp flour
- ✓ 2 cups milk
- ✓ 1/2 c grated provolone cheese
- ✓ salt and pepper to taste

INSTRUCTIONS

01. Make the provolone cheese sauce.

02. In a medium skillet over moderate-low heat, sauté the onions, mushrooms, and bell peppers until tender.

03. Lay out the pizza crust dough on a piece of parchment paper or silicone baking mat. Cut the dough in half.

04. Assemble the Stromboli by spreading on about 2 tbsp of the cheese sauce, 6-8 slices of roast beef, the sautéed vegetables, and 3-4 provolone cheese slices on each piece leaving a 1" border on top and sides.

05. Lightly spray the air fryer basket.

06. Roll the rectangles of dough up into logs, like you would with cinnamon rolls. Pinch the edges together and tuck and pinch the ends under. Brush the tops of the Stromboli with the egg wash. Sprinkle additional cheese over top if desired. Use a sharp knife to gently cut a diagonal slit, every 2 inches, on the top of each Stromboli.

07. Place one of the logs in the air fryer basket. Cook at 340°F/170°C for 8-10 minutes, or until the dough is cooked.

08. Carefully remove from the air fryer basket and cook the other log.

09. Enjoy as is or serve with the provolone cheese sauce.

RECIPE NOTES

The provolone cheese sauce as the base is optional. I think it makes the Stromboli more cheesy, juicy, and delicious. You can omit it as a base on your dough and use it just as a dipping sauce. Or you can omit it altogether.

PROVOLONE CHEESE SAUCE

01 Melt butter in a medium saucepan over medium heat. Let the butter cook for 30 seconds or so to evaporate water. It should bubble up, but don't let the butter brown.

02 Add flour and cook the flour, stirring continuously, for no more than 2 minutes, or until flour turns slightly golden. (This is called white roux, which will thicken the cheese sauce and make it nice and smooth.)

03 Slowly pour in milk into the roux, while whisking the mixture continuously. Once all the milk is added, cook it for another 2-3 minutes or until the mixture comes to a boil.

04 Remove from heat and stir in cheese. Whisk until the cheese is fully melted. Season with salt and pepper to taste.

05 Let it cool and thicken slightly before using.

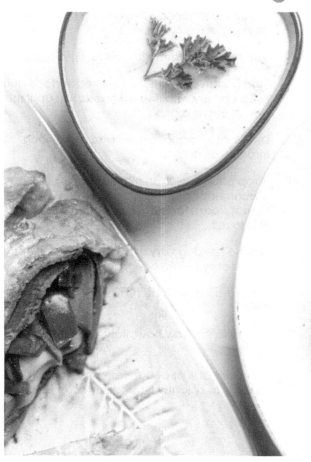

Homemade Corn Dogs

*Homemade corn dogs in the air fryer are healthier and tasty!
The kids will love this one for a quick back-to-school celebration dinner.*

PREP TIME: 30 minutes   **COOK TIME:** 10 minutes   **TOTAL TIME:** 40 minutes   **SERVES:** 8

RECIPE INGREDIENTS

- 1 1/2 c cornmeal (keep it clean with stone ground whole grain)
- 1 1/2 c whole-wheat flour plus 1/3 c of flour, divided
- 3 tbsp organic evaporated cane juice or granulated sugar
- 2 tsp baking powder
- 1/4 tsp baking soda
- 1 tsp onion powder
- 1/4 tsp ground cayenne pepper optional
- 4 tbsp unsalted butter frozen
- 1 c low fat buttermilk (see substitution on page 248)
- 8 hot dogs (keep it clean with all natural uncured nitrite-free beef)
- 2 large egg whites
- 8 wooden skewers soaked in water for 30 minutes

INSTRUCTIONS

01 In a large bowl, whisk cornmeal, 1 1/2 cup of flour, sugar, baking powder, baking soda, onion powder, and cayenne.

02 With the large holes of a box grater, shred the butter over top of flour mixture, stopping 2 or 3 times to toss flour over the butter to prevent clumping.

03 Stir until combined, breaking up any large clumps.

04 Add buttermilk and stir until just moistened.

05 Turn dough onto a lightly floured surface and knead briefly with floured hands just until the dough forms a ball.

06 Divide into 2 equal pieces and press each into a thick disk.

07 Wrap each loosely in plastic wrap or parchment and freeze for 10 minutes. **Note: Do not freeze for longer, or dough will be too stiff to roll.**

08 Pat the hot dogs dry with a paper towel and stick a skewer into each, about 2-3 inches.

09 On a large plate, add remaining 1/3 cup of flour.

10 In a wide, shallow bowl, lightly beat egg whites.

11 Remove 1 disk of dough from the freezer and transfer to a lightly floured surface.

RECIPE NOTES

Remoisten hands between wrapping each hot dog or else the crust becomes too crumbly as you are trying to wrap it around. The moistness ensures that it stays pliable.

You can use wooden coffee stir sticks for the skewers, if needed.

12. Using a lightly floured roller, roll into a 13-inch wide oval, only a scant 1/4 inch thick.

13. Cut into about 4 strips that will wrap around the hot dogs vertically, about 3 inches wide and 4.5 inches tall, depending on the size of the hot dogs.

14. Dip a hot dog in the flour, shaking off excess, and then dip in the egg whites.

15. Using moist hands, wrap the hot dog with dough, gently pushing the seam together to seal.

16. Repeat by dipping and wrapping 3 more hot dogs.

17. Pinch excess dough at ends to completely cover the tip and leave a scant 1/4 inch of hot dog exposed at the skewer end.

18. Repeat the process with remaining disk of dough and 4 more hot dogs.

19. Lightly spray air fryer basket with oil, then place corn dogs into the air fryer (leave space between the corn dogs).

20. Cook at 370°F/187°C for about 10 minutes, flipping halfway through, until crusts are golden brown.

30 Minute Turkey Meatball Subs

Tasty and easy turkey meatball subs your family will love! And they are healthy too! Don't like ground turkey? Sub it with some lean ground beef!

PREP TIME: 15 minutes   **COOK TIME:** 15 minutes   **TOTAL TIME:** 30 minutes   **SERVES:** 6

RECIPE INGREDIENTS

MEATBALLS

- 1 lb ground turkey or beef
- 1 garlic clove minced
- 1/2 tsp onion powder
- 1/2 tsp salt
- 1/2 tsp Italian seasoning
- 1/4 tsp pepper
- 1 egg lightly beaten
- 1/2 c lightly processed oatmeal
- pinch red pepper flakes

OTHER INGREDIENTS

- 1 bell pepper thinly sliced
- 1/2 onion
- 2 c mushrooms halved
- 1/2 tsp Kosher salt
- 6 brioche buns
- favorite white cheese (I used shredded mozzarella)
- marinara sauce
- fresh parsley, dill, or basil to garnish

INSTRUCTIONS

01 Mix meatball ingredients together until well combined.

02 Form meatballs into walnut sized balls, a cookie scoop works great.

03 Lightly spray the air fryer basket with oil and place meatballs in a single layer.

04 Surround the meatballs with the bell pepper, onion, and mushrooms. Sprinkle on 1/2 tsp of Kosher salt and lightly spray the veggies with oil.

05 Cook at 350°F/176°C for 10 minutes stirring once.

06 Remove the meatballs & veggies from the air fryer basket.

07 Place 3 meatballs in a brioche bun with your favorite white cheese and a drizzle of your favorite marinara sauce.

08 Put the brioche bun with the meatballs back in the air fryer for about 1-2 minutes more to toast the bun and melt the cheese.

09 Top with fresh parsley, dill, or basil and enjoy!

Loaded French Fries

These loaded French fries in the air fryer are quick, adaptable, and so tasty too.

PREP TIME: 5 minutes   **COOK TIME:** 20 minutes   **TOTAL TIME:** 25 minutes   **SERVES:** 4

RECIPE INGREDIENTS

- 14 oz frozen French fries
- 1 tbsp taco seasoning
- avocado oil
- 4 oz Cotija cheese grated, see note
- 1/2 medium tomato diced
- 1/2 avocado diced
- 2 green onions sliced

SAUCE

- 1/3 c sour cream (see note)
- 1/2 tsp taco seasoning
- 1/2 tsp Sriracha sauce

RECIPE NOTES

Cheese option: Substitute with Colby Jack cheese if you want fries to stick together more.

Sauce option: You can use mayonnaise instead of sour cream here if you want less of a sour cream sauce and more of a spicy fry sauce.

INSTRUCTIONS

01 Preheat the air fryer at 400°F/200°C for 5 minutes.

02 Place the fries in the air fryer basket. Lightly spray with avocado oil and toss with taco seasoning.

03 Cook at 400°F/200°C for 15 minutes, shaking the basket every 5 minutes.

04 While the fries are cooking, grate the Cotija cheese, whisk together the sauce ingredients, and chop the tomato, avocado, and green onions.

05 Once the fries are finished, remove them from the air fryer basket onto a large plate.

06 Place a sheet of air fryer parchment paper in the basket and place fries back in basket. Sprinkle cheese evenly over top of the fries.

07 Cook for an additional 3-4 minutes at 350°F/176°C or until the cheese is melted.

08 Carefully remove the fries from the parchment paper.

09 Top the fries with tomatoes, avocados, and green onions and sauce.

The Best Fried Mac and Cheese Balls

Cheesy and crunchy fried mac and cheese in the air fryer is healthier and takes half the time!

PREP TIME: 75 minutes   **COOK TIME:** 15 minutes   **TOTAL TIME:** 90 minutes   **SERVES:** 4

RECIPE INGREDIENTS

- 1 lb raw elbow macaroni
- 2 tbsp unsalted butter
- 2 tbsp flour
- 1 1/2 c milk plus 2 tbsp for egg soak
- 1/2 lb grated cheddar
- 1/2 lb grated smoked gouda
- salt and pepper to taste
- 4 large eggs
- 4 c seasoned bread crumbs
- marinara or alfredo sauce for dipping

RECIPE NOTES

Do not overcook noodles, or they will be too mushy to hold a good shape.

You can play with the ratio of cheddar cheese to Gouda cheese to your preference

Use an ice cream scoop to help create uniformed sized balls.

If you wanted to make this ahead, you could freeze the formed cheese balls prior to the coating. Then when you are ready to cook them, remove them from the freezer, coat them in the egg & breadcrumbs as instructed, and then fry them for a little longer since they were originally frozen.

INSTRUCTIONS

01. Cook macaroni al dente according to package instructions. Drain and rinse with cold water. Drain well shaking sieve.

02. While noodles are cooking, melt butter in a saucepan over medium heat. Sprinkle in flour and stir with a whisk until thickened.

03. Whisk in warm milk, working out any lumps. Cook for about 2 minutes until sauce has come to a boil and thickened. Add 1 more tbsp flour if it is not thickened. Remove from heat.

04. Add both cheeses and stir until melted and smooth. Season with salt and pepper.

05. Fold in macaroni and pour into a shallow pan spreading into an even layer and refrigerate for at least 1 hour or until macaroni is cold and set, making it easier to mold into balls.

06. Shape the cold mac and cheese into meatball-sized balls.

07. Beat eggs with 2 tbsp milk and pour into small bowl. Pour the breadcrumbs into a shallow bowl.

08. Dip the balls into the egg then into the bread crumbs. Repeat these steps twice for each ball to give it a thick coating of bread crumbs.

09. Preheat the air fryer. Place the coated mac and cheese balls in a single layer without touching and cook at 380°F/193°C for 10 minutes, until golden brown and center is hot. No need to flip halfway. Serve with your favorite marinara or alfredo sauce for dipping.

Thanksgiving Leftover Hand Pies

Make this any time of the year, but it's a perfect way to repurpose leftovers and save time!!

PREP TIME: 10 minutes   **COOK TIME:** 8 minutes   **TOTAL TIME:** 18 minutes   **SERVES:** 6

RECIPE INGREDIENTS

- ✓ 1 box refrigerator pie crust
- ✓ 1/2 c leftover mashed sweet potatoes (or mashed potatoes)
- ✓ 1 c leftover stuffing
- ✓ 1 c leftover turkey, chopped
- ✓ 1/2 c leftover cranberry sauce
- ✓ 1/2 c leftover gravy
- ✓ 1 egg

INSTRUCTIONS

01. Roll out the pie crust on a lightly floured surface. Use a 6 inch cereal bowl or dough press to make 6 inch circles. Gather the scraps and reroll the dough to get a total of 6 circles from the two pie crusts.

02. On each circle spread out 2 tsp of mashed sweet potatoes. Then top that off with 3 tsp of stuffing and 2 tsp of turkey. Finally add 1 tsp of cranberry sauce and 1 tsp of gravy to each circle.

03. Do not put more than 3 tbsp (9 tsp) of filling in each circle.

04. Use your fingers to run water around the edge of each circle. Fold it in half and crimp it closed tightly with a fork.

05. Put the egg in a bowl and mix with a fork. Use a pastry brush to coat the outside of the hand pies.

06. Cook at 370°F/187°C in an air fryer for 8 minutes. Do not crowd the hand pies in the air fryer and make multiple batches if necessary.

07. Bake until nicely brown. Serve with leftover cranberry sauce and gravy.

Beef Empanadas

The meat mixture is amazing and so tasty! Double the recipe and freeze some to use later for taco night, quesadilla fold over tacos, or MORE empanadas!

PREP TIME: 10 minutes   **COOK TIME:** 17 minutes   **TOTAL TIME:** 27 minutes   **SERVES:** 4

RECIPE INGREDIENTS

- 1 lb ground beef
- 1/2 bell pepper, diced
- 1/4-1/2 onion, diced
- 1 tsp ground cumin
- 1 tsp garlic powder
- 1 tsp oregano
- 1/2 tsp salt
- 1/2 tsp paprika
- 1/2 tsp onion powder
- 1/2 cup (4 oz) tomato sauce
- 2 tbsp water
- discos, pie crust, or Pillsbury biscuit/crescent dough

INSTRUCTIONS

01 Place the ground beef in the air fryer and break it up into chunks. Add the bell pepper and onion on top and cook for 7 minutes at 380°F/193°C, stirring at the halfway point. Drain excess liquids.

02 Sprinkle spices over top, stir well and cook for an additional 2 minutes.

03 Remove the meat from the air fryer basket and pour into a bowl. Add the tomato sauce and water.

04 Place the meat on the discos. I used a roll of Pillsbury French bread dough and cut it into squares about the size of my hand. Place about 2 tbsp of meat mixture on one side of each square. Fold over the dough and use a fork to seal the dough.

05 Lightly spray the air fryer basket and place the empanadas inside.

06 Cover with an egg wash and cook at 350°F/176°C for 6-8 minutes.

Homemade Pizza Bagels

Make Pizza Bagel Bites in the air fryer! This quick little snack can be cooked up in just a few minutes and tastes better than a microwave and won't heat up your kitchen!

PREP TIME: 5 minutes   **COOK TIME:** 5 minutes   **TOTAL TIME:** 10 minutes   **SERVES:** 2

RECIPE INGREDIENTS

- ✓ 2 mini bagels
- ✓ 1/2 c pizza sauce
- ✓ 1 c shredded mozzarella cheese divided
- ✓ pepperoni slices or other desired toppings

INSTRUCTIONS

01. Preheat your air fryer to 400°F/200°C.

02. Separate the bagels, and place them in the basket. Top each bagel half with sauce, cheese and desired toppings.

03. Place in the basket of the air fryer and cook for 5 minutes or until the cheese is melted.

04. Serve immediately.

RECIPE NOTES

To keep pepperoni or other toppings from flying around, place a wire rack over the top of the pizza bagels. Find my favorite rack at AirFryerTools.com.

Margherita Pizza

Enjoy this quick and easy recipe for Margherita Pizza!

PREP TIME: 5 minutes   **COOK TIME:** 8 minutes   **TOTAL TIME:** 13 minutes   **SERVES:** 1

RECIPE INGREDIENTS

- 1 thin crust pre-made cooked pizza crust
- 3 tbsp pizza sauce
- 1 Campari tomato thinly sliced
- 5 slices of fresh mozzarella
- fresh basil
- 1 tsp olive oil

INSTRUCTIONS

01 Spread the pizza sauce over the prepared pizza crust. Place the tomato slices evenly apart on the crust. Add the fresh mozzarella in between the tomato slices.

02 Place in the basket of the air fryer and cook at 350°F/176°C for 5-8 minutes or until the cheese is melted.

03 Remove the pizza from the air fryer and add the fresh basil and olive oil. Serve immediately.

Crunchy "Grilled" Cheese Sandwiches

Check out my new favorite way to make grilled cheese sandwiches!
These grilled cheese sandos are the best!

PREP TIME: 1 minutes   **COOK TIME:** 5 minutes   **TOTAL TIME:** 6 minutes   **SERVES:** 2

RECIPE INGREDIENTS

- 4 pieces thick moist bread
- butter
- 2 slices cheese

RECIPE NOTES

For best results, use a thicker, moister bread, like Grandma Sycamore's brand. If your air fryer fan is too powerful and is blowing the bread off the top, try inserting a few toothpicks to keep it from blowing off or place a rack over top.

INSTRUCTIONS

01 Butter one side of each slice of bread. Place two of the bread slices in the air fryer, buttered side down. Place cheese on each of the bread slices, then top with the second slice of bread, buttered side up.

02 Cook at 350°F/176°C for 6-8 minutes, flipping halfway through cooking. If you want a little more toasting, turn the air fryer up to 400°F/200°C for an additional 1-2 minutes.

03 Serve warm. Perfect for dipping in soup!

Loaded Nachos

This loaded nachos recipe is super fast if you have some leftover taco meat.
Whip it up after school for a quick, fun snack.

PREP TIME: 20 minutes   **COOK TIME:** 5 minutes   **TOTAL TIME:** 25 minutes   **SERVES:** 2

RECIPE INGREDIENTS

- 1 lb cooked ground beef
- 1 packet taco seasoning
- 3 oz tortilla chips
- black beans
- 8 oz grated Colby/Jack Cheese
- Pico de gallo or salsa
- avocado, sliced
- sour cream
- chopped cilantro
- sliced scallions

INSTRUCTIONS

01 Preheat air fryer to 400°F/200°C for 5 minutes.

02 Combine the cooked ground beef with taco seasoning.

03 Line the bottom of air fryer basket with a 9x9 piece of parchment or foil.

04 Place the chips, 1/2 of the meat, black beans, and cheese on the parchment. Or use the amount of topping you prefer. Reserve any remaining toppings for another batch.

05 Cook for 3 to 4 minutes at 330°F/165°C, until the cheese is melted.

06 Carefully slide the parchment out of the basket and onto a plate. Top with Pico de gallo or salsa, avocado, sour cream, cilantro, and scallions. Repeat with the remaining half of the ingredients.

Pigs in a Blanket

A classic favorite that cooks so fast in the air fryer!

PREP TIME: 35 minutes   COOK TIME: 6 minutes   TOTAL TIME: 41 minutes   SERVES: 3-4

RECIPE INGREDIENTS

- ✓ 8 oz cocktail sausages
- ✓ 1 sheet puff pastry
- ✓ 1/4 c honey mustard (see homemade recipe on page 248)
- ✓ 1 tbsp bagel seasoning
- ✓ 1 egg, lightly beaten – optional

INSTRUCTIONS

01 Defrost the puff pastry enough to unfold it but so it's still firm and chilled, about 30 minutes. Use a sharp knife or pizza cutter to cut the puff pastry into 2 x 4 inch pieces.

02 Preheat the air fryer to 400°F/200°C.

03 Pat the sausages dry with paper towels. Spoon 1/2 tsp of honey mustard onto the end of each piece of puff pastry, and place a cocktail sausage on top of each.

04 Gently roll the puff pastry around the sausage, pressing to seal together at the end. Set it seam side down on the board. Brush the top of the puff pastry with egg and sprinkle with bagel seasoning.

05 Set 10-15 pigs in a blanket in your air fryer basket, seam side down, leaving a little space between each one so the air can circulate. Cook for 5-6 minutes, until flakey and crispy. Serve with extra honey mustard or ketchup.

Crunchy Plantain Chips

*Tasty air fryer plantain chips that are just as good
as the ones you'd buy from Trader Joe's*

PREP TIME: 5 minutes   **COOK TIME:** 25 minutes   **TOTAL TIME:** 30 minutes   **SERVES:** 4

RECIPE INGREDIENTS

- ✅ 1 large green plantain
- ✅ 1 tbsp sugar
- ✅ 1 tsp cinnamon

RECIPE NOTES

The plantain does not have to be
super green, it can be semi-ripe.

INSTRUCTIONS

01. Peel the plantain and cut it into uniform slices, about 1/8 inch to 1/4 inch in thickness.

02. Spray basket bottom with avocado oil. Place slices in the basket and spray the tops lightly with oil.

03. Cook at 350°F/176°C for 5 minutes. Carefully take out, transfer to a cutting board, and smash the slices flat using a flat spatula, small skillet, or a drinking glass - anything flat will work.

04. Carefully return slices to the fryer basket in a single layer and air fry another 5 minutes at 350°F/176°C.

05. Lightly spray with avocado spray again, then sprinkle with cinnamon and sugar, salt, or the seasoning of your choice.

06. Cook at 200°F/93°C for up to 15 minutes, checking occasionally until they are dried, removing them as they are done.

07. Allow to cool completely. Store in a sealed container on the counter for up to 10 days.

Yummy Homemade Tortilla Chips

*Quick and easy homemade tortilla chips in the air fryer
at a fraction of the cost.*

PREP TIME: 5 minutes   **COOK TIME:** 8 minutes   **TOTAL TIME:** 13 minutes   **SERVES:** 2

RECIPE INGREDIENTS

- ✓ 4 small thin corn tortillas
- ✓ avocado oil
- ✓ salt to taste

INSTRUCTIONS

01 Cut the tortillas into fourths.

02 Lightly spray the air fryer basket with oil of your choice.

03 Layer the tortilla chips inside the air fryer basket, it's okay if they overlap. Lightly spray with oil.

04 If you are worried about the chips blowing around, take your air fryer accessory rack and place it on top of the chips.

05 Cook at 330°F/165°C for 6-8 minutes, turning once or until they reach desired crispiness.

Avocado Fries

Crunchy, creamy, and healthy! You will love these Keto friendly avocado fries!

PREP TIME: 13 minutes   **COOK TIME:** 12 minutes   **TOTAL TIME:** 25 minutes   **SERVES:** 4

RECIPE INGREDIENTS

- 2 large firm avocados or 3 small firm avocados
- 1 c crushed pork rinds
- 1 tsp salt
- 1/2 tsp garlic powder
- 1/2 tsp onion powder
- 2 large eggs beaten

RECIPE NOTES

Make sure you buy firm avocados and use them within a couple days of purchase, otherwise they will become too mushy to peel or slice.

INSTRUCTIONS

01. Preheat your air fryer to 400°F/200°C.

02. Slice the avocados in half lengthwise and remove the pit. Peel the skin off of the flesh and cut the avocado into 1/2 to 1 inch slices lengthwise.

03. In a shallow bowl, mix the crushed pork rinds with the seasonings. Place beaten eggs in a separate shallow bowl.

04. Coat each slice of avocado in the egg, followed by the pork rind mixture. Repeat these steps with each of your slices patting coating on gently and set them aside on a plate.

05. Spray the inside of your air fryer with cooking spray and place your coated avocado slices inside your basket.

06. Cook the avocado fries at 400°F/200°C for 12 minutes. No need to flip halfway through.

Homemade Pullman Bread

Making homemade bread in the air fryer is incredibly easy and means you don't have to heat up your kitchen!

PREP TIME: 120 minutes   **COOK TIME:** 30 minutes   **TOTAL TIME:** 150 minutes   **SERVES:** 6

RECIPE INGREDIENTS

- ✔ 3 c all-purpose flour (384 g)
- ✔ 1/2 c milk, room temperature (123 g)
- ✔ 1/2 c lukewarm water (118 g)
- ✔ 4 tbsp butter, room temperature (56 g)
- ✔ 2 tbsp sugar (25 g)
- ✔ 1 1/2 tsp salt (7 g)
- ✔ 2 1/4 tsp instant yeast (8 g)

RECIPE NOTES

This recipe was shared by viewer, Richard, and he used a Pullman loaf pan. For a basket style air fryer, you would use two mini Pullman loaf pans, that are 2.8"x8.1"x2.8". Alternatively, you can use any loaf pan that will fit in your air fryer. Just cover with foil to keep the top from burning. Remove the foil during the last 5 minutes of cooking. Find the pan I used at AirFryerTools.com.

INSTRUCTIONS

01 Add all ingredients to a stand mixing bowl fitted with a dough hook. Mix well until dough comes together then knead for 5-6 minutes. Dough should be soft, smooth, elastic, and tacky. Or place in a bread maker in order given and follow instructions for dough.

02 Remove dough and knead by hand and form into a ball. Lightly spray the bowl with an oil spray and place the ball of dough back into the bowl. Cover with plastic wrap or a clean towel and let rise for 1-2 hours or until doubled.

03 Punch down dough to remove air bubbles. (Divide dough equally if using two pans). Roll out dough, keeping with the width of the loaf pan, and roll up the dough tightly, pinching the seam and tucking the ends under. Place loaf in a lightly sprayed/greased Pullman loaf pan. Cover and let rise for another 30 minutes.

04 Bake covered with a loaf pan lid at 370°F/187°C for 21-22 minutes (for two smaller pans) or 30 minutes (for larger pan), until internal temperature reaches 200°F/93°C. Turn bread out from pans and let cool on a cooling rack.

Garlic Cheese Keto 'Bread'

*Cheesy garlic bread in the air fryer is a great keto snack
that is packed with tasty ingredients you will love!*

PREP TIME: 5 minutes   **COOK TIME:** 10 minutes   **TOTAL TIME:** 15 minutes   **SERVES:** 2

RECIPE INGREDIENTS

- 1 c shredded mozzarella cheese
- 1/3 c freshly grated parmesan, + 1 tbsp more for topping
- 1 egg lightly beaten
- 1/2 tsp Italian seasoning
- 1/2 tsp garlic powder
- 1/2 tsp parsley for garnish, optional

INSTRUCTIONS

01. Preheat the air fryer at 350°F/176°C for at least 5 minutes while you put the recipe together.

02. Spray a 6" pizza pan with avocado oil.

03. Mix all ingredients together and spread evenly in pan.

04. Place in air fryer basket and cook at 350°F/176°C for 3 minutes, checking after 2 minutes, looking for the top to get golden brown, rotating pan as needed for even browning.

05. Take it out and cool in the pan for 2 minutes. Heat air fryer at 350°F/176°C for 2 minutes.

06. Carefully turn bread over with a spatula or silicone turner. Put back in fryer for another 2-3 minutes till top is golden, rotating as needed each minute.

07. Sprinkle with remaining parmesan cheese, then cook for about 2 more minutes at 350°F/176°C till the top is melted the way you want it. Top with parsley.

08. Cool in pan for several minutes, then serve from the pan or transfer to a plate. As it cools it will become more bread-like.

Garlic Bread

Toast up a yummy side of garlic bread in your air fryer to complement any Italian themed dinner!

PREP TIME: 5 minutes   **COOK TIME:** 5 minutes   **TOTAL TIME:** 10 minutes   **SERVES:** 4

RECIPE INGREDIENTS

- ✓ 1 baguette
- ✓ melted butter
- ✓ seasonings such as garlic powder, Italian seasoning, and salt

INSTRUCTIONS

01. Cut the baguette into desired slices. You can make them long or short, either works!

02. Butter and season each baguette slice.

03. Cook at 350°F/175°C for 4-6 minutes.

Baked Rhodes Rolls

Pre-made frozen rolls in the air fryer can be whipped up in no time! If your store doesn't carry Rhodes Rolls, you can use this same method using your favorite homemade roll dough recipe!

PREP TIME: 6 minutes   **COOK TIME:** 15 minutes   **TOTAL TIME:** 21 minutes   **SERVES:** 6

RECIPE INGREDIENTS

- ✓ 9 Rhodes Rolls, thawed
- ✓ 2 tbsp butter, melted
- ✓ garlic salt, to taste(optional)

INSTRUCTIONS

01. Preheat the air fryer at 400°F/200°C for 5 minutes.

02. Place 9 thawed balls of dough on parchment paper in the air fryer, drizzle with melted butter. Close the air fryer basket and let the dough balls rise for 20-30 minutes. Make sure the air fryer stays off.

03. When rolls have risen to desired size, cook in the air fryer at 320°F/160°C for 8-10 min, or until the rolls are cooked through and browned on top.

Stuffed Mini Peppers

Make these adorable and delicious stuffed mini peppers in your air fryer. They are the perfect appetizer for a game day get-together or as a fun afternoon snack.

PREP TIME: 7 minutes   **COOK TIME:** 8 minutes   **TOTAL TIME:** 15 minutes   **SERVES:** 6

RECIPE INGREDIENTS

- ✅ 6 mini sweet peppers
- ✅ 8 oz cream cheese
- ✅ Everything But The Bagel Seasoning, to taste

INSTRUCTIONS

01. Wash the peppers, cut them in half lengthwise, and clean out the middle.
02. Pat the peppers dry.
03. Fill the peppers with cream cheese.
04. Place a piece of parchment paper inside the air fryer basket. Place the peppers on top.
05. Sprinkle each of the peppers with Everything But The Bagel Seasoning to taste.
06. Air fryer at 380°F/193°C for 8 minutes. Remove from the air fryer basket and enjoy!

Crispy Chickpeas Snack

Air fryer chickpeas are a very healthy snack! And so simple and delicious!

PREP TIME: 3 minutes   **COOK TIME:** 12 minutes   **TOTAL TIME:** 15 minutes   **SERVES:** 2

RECIPE INGREDIENTS

- ✓ 15 oz can chickpeas, (garbanzo beans), rinsed well and drained
- ✓ 1/8 tsp garlic powder
- ✓ 1/8 tsp onion powder
- ✓ 1/8 tsp cinnamon
- ✓ 1/8 tsp smoked paprika or regular paprika

RECIPE NOTES

To store the chickpeas, place them in a loosely sealed plastic bag lined with a paper towel or in a paper towel.

INSTRUCTIONS

01 Drain the chickpeas well.

02 Place a single layer of the chickpeas in the air fryer basket and cook at 390°F/198°C for 5 minutes to dry out the chickpeas.

03 Spray the chickpeas with oil. If you don't have an oil sprayer, pour a little bit of oil on beans and stir with a silicone spoon.

04 Cook for an additional 5 minutes in the air fryer.

05 Mix together the garlic powder, onion powder, cinnamon, and smoked paprika in a small bowl to make the seasoning.

06 Add 1/2 of the seasoning to the chickpeas. Stir well.

07 Cook for an additional 2 minutes (or until crisped to your liking).

08 Carefully take the chickpeas out of the air fryer. Toss with the remaining seasoning and enjoy!

Toasted Uncrustables

*Enjoy this fun twist on Uncrustables! It makes for
a quick and tasty midday or midnight snack!*

PREP TIME: 0 minutes   **COOK TIME:** 5 minutes   **TOTAL TIME:** 5 minutes   **SERVES:** 4

RECIPE INGREDIENTS

- 4 Uncrustables sandwiches
- Nutella to taste

INSTRUCTIONS

01. Place the frozen Uncrustables in the air fryer basket.

02. Cook at 370°F/187°C for 5 minutes.

03. Top with Nutella and enjoy!

Apple Chips

*Make a delicious and healthy afternoon
snack in your air fryer with these apple chips.*

PREP TIME: 5 minutes   **COOK TIME:** 20 minutes   **TOTAL TIME:** 25 minutes   **SERVES:** 4

RECIPE INGREDIENTS

- ✅ 4 apples sliced 1/8"
  with a mandolin or
  kitchen knife.

- ✅ 1 tsp cinnamon

RECIPE NOTES

Cooking time and temp may
vary according to air fryer.
Watch your apples closely.

INSTRUCTIONS

01. Place apples in an air fryer basket and
    sprinkle with cinnamon.

02. Cook at 300°F/150°C for 10 minutes, then turn
    apples over and cook for an additional 10
    minutes or until they reach desired crispness.

Beef Jerky

This beef jerky is easier and more delicious than you'll expect! Give it a try!

PREP TIME: 5 minutes   **COOK TIME:** 60 minutes   **TOTAL TIME:** 65 minutes   **SERVES:** 8

RECIPE INGREDIENTS

- 1 lb flank steak sliced 1/8-inch thick and cut into strips
- 2 tbsp soy sauce
- 1 tbsp Worcestershire sauce
- 1 tbsp liquid smoke
- 1 tbsp brown sugar
- 1 tsp salt
- 1/2 tsp pepper
- 1/2 tsp meat tenderizer
- 1/2 tsp garlic powder
- 1/2 tsp onion powder
- 1/2 tsp paprika

INSTRUCTIONS

01 Whisk together the soy sauce, Worcestershire, liquid smoke, brown sugar, salt, pepper, meat tenderizer, garlic powder, onion powder, and paprika. Add meat to sauce and let marinate for about 8 hours.

02 Remove meat from marinade and pat meat dry with paper towels. Arrange meat in single layers in the air fryer using racks to create layers. Air fry at 180°F/82°C for 45 minutes. Check it, then add 15-25 more minutes until it reaches your desired texture. Cook longer for a tougher chewier jerky. (60 minutes was just about right for me).

Avocado Egg Rolls - Cheesecake Factory Copycat

Easy, simple, and amazing: this Cheesecake Factory
Copycat avocado egg rolls will be ready and eaten in no time!

PREP TIME: 10 minutes   **COOK TIME:** 8 minutes   **TOTAL TIME:** 18 minutes   **SERVES:** 4

RECIPE INGREDIENTS

- 2 small avocados
- 1/4 c cilantro chopped
- 1/4 c red onion diced
- 2 tbsp sun dried tomatoes diced
- 1/2 lime juice
- 1/2 tsp Kosher salt
- 1/4 tsp black pepper
- 1/2 tsp chili pepper
- 1/8 tsp garlic powder
- 4 egg roll wrappers full sized

AVOCADO DIP

- 1 1/2-2 tbsp sour cream
- 1 tbsp non-fat Greek yogurt
- 1 small avocado
- 1/2 lime juiced about 2 tsp
- 1/4 tsp kosher salt
- 1/8 tsp black pepper
- cayenne pepper to taste

INSTRUCTIONS

01. Mix together diced avocado, cilantro, red onion, sun dried tomatoes, lime juice, salt, pepper, chili powder and garlic powder in a bowl.

02. Divide mixture into four sections. Add 1/4 of the avocado egg roll mixture into the middle of four egg roll wrappers, placing the wrapper in a diamond position, so one point is facing at the bottom.

03. Using a small amount of water, moisten the four outside edges with water (only about 1/4 inch, just to moisten so the outer edges will stick).

04. Fold bottom corner up and over the filling and then each side, one by one, over each other, being sure to moisten each edge with water so it sticks closed.

05. Roll completely closed and moisten any open edges so they stay closed. Finish the other three egg rolls and then spray each side with cooking spray.

06. Preheat the air fryer to 400°F/200°C. When ready, place sprayed egg rolls into the air fryer basket.

07. Cook at 400°F/200°C for 8 minutes, flipping halfway through.

08. While cooking, mix together avocado dip ingredients in a food processor. If you don't have a food processor, you can whip everything together with a fork until combined and smooth.

09. When egg rolls are finished, cut each in half and serve with avocado dipping sauce for a delicious appetizer, snack, or side.

French Bread Pizza

Here's an easy way to make pizza for a quick weekend snack or lunch!

PREP TIME: 5 minutes   **COOK TIME:** 8 minutes   **TOTAL TIME:** 13 minutes   **SERVES:** 2

RECIPE INGREDIENTS

- French bread
- Favorite pizza sauce and toppings

INSTRUCTIONS

01. Slice the french bread in half and again lengthwise.
02. Butter the bread and toast in the air fryer at 350°F/176°C for 3-4 minutes.
03. Dress the pizza with your favorite sauce and toppings.
04. Bake in the air fryer for an additional 4 minutes.

Roasted Apples

A quick and easy dessert - enjoy on ice cream or as is!

PREP TIME: 10 minutes   **COOK TIME:** 8 minutes   **TOTAL TIME:** 18 minutes   **SERVES:** 4

RECIPE INGREDIENTS

- 1-2 large apples
- 2 tbsp melted butter
- 2-3 tbps brown sugar
- cinnamon, to taste

INSTRUCTIONS

01. Cube the apples. Place apples in a bowl.
02. Coat with the melted butter, brown sugar, and cinnamon.
03. Place apples in the air fryer and level out.
04. Bake at 350°F/176°C for 8 minutes, stirring at the halfway point.

Zucchini Pizza Bites

A healthier way to have "pizza" that tastes delightfully good!

PREP TIME: 10 minutes   **COOK TIME:** 12 minutes   **TOTAL TIME:** 22 minutes   **SERVES:** 4

RECIPE INGREDIENTS

- 1/2 zucchini
- salt, to taste
- garlic powder, to taste
- your favorite pizza sauce and toppings

INSTRUCTIONS

01 Cut the zucchini into 1/2 inch thick slices. Lightly season with the salt and garlic powder.

02 Cook at 320°F/160°C for 8 minutes.

03 Top the zucchini slices with pizza sauce, cheese, and other desired pizza toppings.

04 Cook at 400°F/200°C for an additional 3 minutes, or until the cheese is melted.

Roasted Garlic

If you have a recipe that calls for roasted garlic, save yourself time and money and prep your garlic this way!

PREP TIME: 10 minutes   **COOK TIME:** 12 minutes   **TOTAL TIME:** 22 minutes   **SERVES:** 4

RECIPE INGREDIENTS

- bulb of garlic

INSTRUCTIONS

01 Cut off the top part of the garlic bulb and remove the garlic skins.

02 Wrap the garlic in tin foil. Before closing the garlic, lightly spray the contents with avocado oil. Cover the garlic completely in tin foil.

03 Place in the air fryer basket and cook for 20-30 minutes at 390°F/195°C.

04 Let the garlic cool slightly. Then, squeeze the garlic out of its remaining skin to enjoy.

Dorito Cheese Bites

A fun twist on the traditional fried mozzarella cheese stick!

PREP TIME: 1 hour 10 minutes **COOK TIME:** 6 minutes **TOTAL TIME:** 1 hour 16 minutes **SERVES:** 6

RECIPE INGREDIENTS

- 3/4 c flour, divided
- 1-2 eggs
- 1 c crushed Doritos, about 3-4 handfuls of chips
- 5-6 Babybel cheese, frozen

INSTRUCTIONS

01 Freeze unwrapped Babybel cheeses for a few hours.

02 Set up your stations. In one bowl, 1/2 cup of flour. In a second bowl, 1-2 eggs, whisked. In a third bowl, 1/4 cup of flour and crushed Doritos, mixed together.

03 Dip the cheese in the flour, the egg wash, the Doritos mix, the egg wash, and then the Doritos mix again.

04 Place in a lightly greased air fryer basket.

05 Lightly spray the tops of the cheese bites and cook in the air fryer at 380°F/193°C for 6 minutes, flipping at the halfway point.

Hot Dogs

NEVER use that microwave for heating up hot dogs again! Air fried hot dogs are the way to go!

PREP TIME: 0 minutes **COOK TIME:** 5 minutes **TOTAL TIME:** 5 minutes **SERVES:** 4

RECIPE INGREDIENTS

- 4 hot dogs
- 4 hot dogs buns

INSTRUCTIONS

01 Place in the air fryer basket and cook at 350°F/175°C for 3-4 minutes, or until cooked through.

02 Take it one step further and place the hot dogs inside hot dog bun and cook for an additional minute or two.

Homemade Croutons

You'll never use store bought croutons again!

PREP TIME: 10 minutes   **COOK TIME:** 12 minutes   **TOTAL TIME:** 22 minutes   **SERVES:** 4

RECIPE INGREDIENTS

- 2 slices of white bread, or other bread of your choice
- avocado oil
- salt, to taste
- pepper, to taste
- garlic powder, to taste

INSTRUCTIONS

01 Cube the bread into crouton sized pieces.

02 Place the bread in the air fryer basket and lightly spray with oil. Season with salt, pepper, and garlic powder.

03 Cover the bread cubes with a wire rack from an air fryer accessory kit to avoid having the croutons blowing inside the air fryer basket.

04 Cook at 370°F/185°C for 5 minutes, or until golden brown.

Eggplant Parmesan Bites

*Make these as bites, or the traditional slices! Either way,
you'll be surprised at how delicious these are!*

PREP TIME: 15 minutes   **COOK TIME:** 12 minutes   **TOTAL TIME:** 27 minutes   **SERVES:** 6

RECIPE INGREDIENTS

- 1 large eggplant
- 1/4 tsp sea salt
- 2 c panko breadcrumbs or almond flour
- 1/2 c parmesan cheese, fresh or grated
- 1 tbsp Italian seasoning
- 2 tsp garlic powder
- 1 tsp sea salt
- 1 pinch of red pepper flakes, optional
- 2 eggs

INSTRUCTIONS

01. Cut the eggplant into 1 inch cubes and sprinkle on a 1/4 tsp of sea salt. Let the eggplant sweat while you complete the next steps.

02. Combine the panko crumbs with the parmesan cheese, Italian seasoning, garlic powder, salt salt, and red pepper flakes into a shallow dish or plate.

03. Whisk together the 2 eggs in another shallow bowl.

04. Dip the eggplant cubes into the egg wash then the breading mixture.

05. Place bites in a lightly sprayed air fryer basket. Spray the tops of the cubes with avocado oil and cook at 380°F/193°C for 12 minutes, stirring at the halfway point.

06. Remove from the air fryer and enjoy with your favorite marinara sauce.

DESSERTS

Healthier Beignets

Quick, easy, and healthy air fryer beignets are one
of the best desserts to make in the air fryer!

PREP TIME: 140 minutes   **COOK TIME:** 6 minutes   **TOTAL TIME:** 146 minutes   **SERVES:** 8

RECIPE INGREDIENTS

DOUGH

- 3/4 c warm water
- 1/4 c sugar
- 1 tbsp yeast
- 1/2 tsp salt
- 2 tbsp unsalted butter room temperature
- 1 egg beaten
- 1/2 c of milk
- 2 1/2-3 c flour
- 1/4 c melted butter
- 1/2 c powdered sugar

RASPBERRY DIPPING SAUCE

- 1/4 c raspberry jam
- 1-2 tbsp water

INSTRUCTIONS

01 Combine warm water, 1 tbsp sugar, and yeast in a medium bowl.

02 Mix and let it rest for 4-5 minutes, until bubbly.

03 Add salt, butter, egg, and milk. Stir well.

04 Add 1 cup of flour by hand or in a stand mixer with a dough hook. Stir until incorporated.

05 Gradually stir in as much of the remaining flour, until the dough begins to stay together in a ball and a moderately stiff dough is formed.

06 Knead for 5 more minutes.

07 Place dough in an oiled bowl, turn to coat with oil and let it rise for 2 hours covered with a clean towel or plastic wrap.

08 Once the dough has doubled, punch down and roll it into a large rectangle, 1/2 inch thick.

09 Cut the dough into 2x3 inch diamond shapes.

10 Preheat the air fryer at 400°F/200°C for 5 minutes.

11 Dip each rectangle into the 1/4 cup melted butter, then place it in the air fryer basket.

12 Bake at 350°F/176°C for 6 minutes, flipping at the halfway point.

13 Remove to a warm plate and dust with powdered sugar.

14 Mix together raspberry jam and water until combined and serve with beignets.

The Easiest 2 Ingredient Donuts

Enjoy these air fryer donuts in just
15 minutes with this easy two-ingredient dough!

PREP TIME: 8 minutes   **COOK TIME:** 7 minutes   **TOTAL TIME:** 15 minutes   **SERVES:** 4

RECIPE INGREDIENTS

- ✅ 1 c self-rising flour (see substitution on page 248)
- ✅ 3/4 c Greek yogurt plain or vanilla

RECIPE NOTES

Cooking time may vary depending on your air fryer.

My favorite donut glaze recipe: 2 tbsp butter, melted, 1/2 cup powdered sugar, 1/2 tsp vanilla, and 1/2 tbsp hot water.

INSTRUCTIONS

01. Mix the self-rising flour and yogurt together until shaggy, then knead in the bowl until dough is well combined and slightly sticky. The dough will be sticky, but should still be able to form into a ball and not stick to your hands too much.

02. Divide dough into 4 equal pieces. Roll each piece into long ropes (about 9 inches long and 1 inch in diameter). Bring ends together and pinch.

03. Spray the air fryer basket with cooking oil. Place the donuts in the air fryer, with space between them. Spray donuts lightly with cooking spray. Cook in air fryer for 7 minutes at 350°F/176°C, flipping halfway through, until golden brown.

04. Let cool a few minutes, then top with melted butter and cinnamon/sugar, or glaze, or other favorite donut topping (find my favorite donut glaze recipe on page 203).

Donuts + Donut Holes with Sweet Glaze

These are pretty much the closest thing you'll get to Krispy Kreme original glazed donuts! This recipe is so delicious, fun, and easy to make!

PREP TIME: 100 minutes   **COOK TIME:** 16 minutes   **TOTAL TIME:** 116 minutes   **SERVES:** 12

RECIPE INGREDIENTS

- 1 c milk warmed to about 110°F (240 g)
- 2 1/2 tsp active dry yeast or instant yeast (8 g)
- 1/4 c sugar plus 1 tsp (54 g)
- 1/2 tsp kosher salt (3 g)
- 1 large egg
- 4 tbsp unsalted butter (57 g)
- 3 c all-purpose flour (384 g)
- avocado oil

GLAZE

- 6 tbsp unsalted butter (85 g)
- 2 c powdered sugar (224 g)
- 2 tsp vanilla extract (8 g)
- 2-4 tbsp hot water (29-58 g)

INSTRUCTIONS

01 In a large bowl or bowl of a stand mixer (fitted with dough hook), combine the warm milk, 1 tsp sugar, and the yeast. Let sit for about 5-10 minutes, until foamy.

02 Meanwhile, melt the butter and lightly beat the egg.

03 Add remaining 1/4 cup sugar, salt, and egg to the yeast mixture; stir or whisk to combine. Then mix in the melted butter and 2 cups of flour on low speed.

04 Scrape down the sides of bowl, then mix in remaining 1 cup flour. Dough should start to pull away from sides of bowl, but still be sticky (can add up to 1/4 cup flour more, if needed). Increase speed to medium-low and knead for 5 minutes. Dough will become smoother and elastic, but still sticky.

05 Remove dough hook or transfer dough to a greased bowl, turn to coat, cover with plastic wrap. Let rise until doubled about 1-1 1/2 hours (with instant yeast, this will be closer to 30 minutes).

06 Punch down dough and turn out on a lightly floured surface. Gently roll out dough until a little less than 1/2-inch thick. Cut out as many donuts as you can with a round cutter, about 3 inches in diameter. Use a cutter about 1 inch in diameter to cut out the centers.

07 Transfer cut out dough to a lightly greased parchment paper or silicone mat. Cover loosely with greased plastic wrap. Let rise until doubled, about 20-30 minutes.

08 Preheat air fryer to 350°F/176°C. Lightly spray air fryer basket with oil. Carefully transfer donuts to basket in a single layer leaving space around each donut. Lightly spray donuts with oil spray and cook until lightly golden brown, about 4 minutes. Cooking time will vary depending on your air fryer and the thickness of your donuts, so keep an eye on it! Repeat with remaining donuts, then with the donut holes. Transfer donuts to a cooling rack.

09 **Glaze:** While donuts are in the air fryer, melt butter for the glaze in a medium bowl or saucepan. Stir or whisk in the powdered sugar and vanilla, until smooth. Stir or whisk in the hot water 1 tbsp at a time until it reaches desired consistency, somewhat thin but not watery.

10 While donuts are still warm, but after cooling for a few minutes, submerge each into the glaze. For donut holes, glaze last and just dump them into the bowl and gently stir to coat.

11 Move cooling rack over the parchment paper used earlier or a piece of foil to make cleanup easier. Place the glazed donuts on the rack to allow excess to drip off and let sit until glaze hardens, about 10 minutes.

Donuts with Jelly or Cream Filling

Air fryer donuts with a jelly or cream filling?
Yes, please! This recipe is so simple and so tasty!

PREP TIME: 100 minutes   **COOK TIME:** 12 minutes   **TOTAL TIME:** 112 minutes   **SERVES:** 12

RECIPE INGREDIENTS

DOUGH

- 1 c milk (warmed to 110°F) (240g)
- 2 1/2 tsp active dry yeast or instant yeast (8 g)
- 1/4 c sugar plus 1 tsp (54g)
- 1/2 tsp kosher salt (3 g)
- 1 large egg
- 4 tbsp unsalted butter (57 g)
- 3 c all-purpose flour (384g)
- oil spray

SUGAR COATINGS

- 1/2 c sugar or
- 1/2 c sugar with finely grated zest from 1 lemon, (yellow part only)

JAM FILLING

- 1-2 c raspberry jam or other jam of your choice

LEMON CREAM FILLING

- 1 c whipping cream
- 1 tbsp powdered sugar
- 1/4 c lemon curd

INSTRUCTIONS

01. In a large bowl or bowl of a stand mixer (fitted with dough hook), combine the warm milk, 1 tsp sugar, and the yeast. Let sit for about 5-10 minutes, until foamy.

02. Meanwhile, melt the butter and lightly beat the egg.

03. Add remaining 1/4 cup sugar, salt, and egg to the yeast mixture; stir or whisk to combine. Then mix in the melted butter and 2 cups of flour on low speed.

04. Scrape down the sides of bowl, then mix in remaining 1 cup flour. Dough should start to pull away from sides of bowl, but still be sticky (add up to 1/4 cup flour more, if needed). Increase speed to medium-low and knead for 5 minutes. Dough will become smoother and elastic, but still sticky.

05. Remove dough hook or transfer dough to a greased bowl turning to coat, cover with plastic wrap and let rise until doubled, about 1-1 1/2 hours (with instant yeast, this will probably take about 30 minutes).

06. Punch down dough and turn out on lightly floured surface. Gently roll out dough until a little less than 1/2-inch thick, between 1/4-inch and 1/2-inch.

07. Since the donuts won't have a hole, cut circles about 3 inches in diameter.

08. Place dough rounds on parchment paper to rise again. Lightly cover it with plastic wrap until it has doubled (about 30 minutes).

LEMON ZEST SUGAR COATING

01 In a small bowl, mix 1/2 cup sugar and the zest from 1 lemon with a fork breaking up lumps, until well combined. Keep stirring as needed as the oil from the zest makes it sticky and clumps the sugar together.

LEMON CREAM FILLING

01 Whip the cream to soft peaks then beat in powdered sugar. Fold in the lemon curd until smooth.

JAM FILLING

01 Stir jam until it is smooth. You may want to add a little water to the jam to help smooth it out. You can also warm up the jam in the microwave for a couple seconds.

09 Spray air fryer basket with oil, place donuts inside (about 4-5) and spray the tops with oil.

10 Cook at 350°F/176°C for 5 minutes, flip donuts at the 3 minute mark.

11 Take donuts out of the air fryer and coat in sugar. If the sugar isn't sticking to the donuts, lightly spray or brush the donuts in oil and try again.

12 Let them cool completely.

13 To fill the donuts, spoon the filling of choice into a pastry bag with a plain tip. Poke the tip into the side of the doughnut and pipe in the filling until the filling pushes back.

Quick and Easy Cake Donuts

Try these air fryer baked donuts! So quick, easy, and delicious, they are ready in less than 20 minutes. Note: You will need an air fryer silicone donut pan for this recipe.

PREP TIME: 10 minutes   **COOK TIME:** 10 minutes   **TOTAL TIME:** 20 minutes   **SERVES:** 8

RECIPE INGREDIENTS

- 1 c all-purpose flour (120g)
- 1 tsp baking powder
- 1/2 tsp salt
- 1/2 tsp cinnamon
- 1/8 tsp nutmeg
- 1 large egg room temperature
- 1/3 c brown sugar (65 g)
- 1/4 c milk, room temperature (60ml)
- 1/4 c plain yogurt (or Greek yogurt or sour cream), room temperature
- 2 tbsp unsalted butter, melted (30g)
- 1 1/2 tsp vanilla

CINNAMON SUGAR COATING

- 4 tbsp unsalted butter melted
- 3/4 c granulated sugar
- 3/4 tsp cinnamon

INSTRUCTIONS

01. In a large bowl, whisk together the flour, baking powder, salt, cinnamon, and nutmeg. In a medium bowl, lightly beat egg. Whisk in brown sugar, milk, and yogurt, until smooth. Add melted butter and vanilla. Pour wet ingredients into dry ingredients and stir until just combined. Don't over mix.

02. Pipe or spoon batter in 3-inch silicone donut mold.

03. Preheat air fryer at 400°F/200°C for 2-3 minutes. Place donut mold in air fryer and bake at 330°F/165°C for 6 minutes, or until internal temperature of donuts reads above 160°F.

04. Remove mold from air fryer and let cool for 2 minutes, then carefully remove donuts from the mold.

05. Dip the rounded side of the donuts into the melted butter, then the cinnamon sugar mixture. Place coated donuts sugar side up, in air fryer for another 2 minutes at 350°F/176°C.

06. For donut bites: Use muffin bites pan, but don't fill the center cavity. Cook at 350°F/176°C for 6 minutes. Cooking time may vary because muffin bites pans vary in size.

Low Carb Donuts

Enjoy a quick and easy Keto dessert that the whole family will love!
Note: You will need an air fryer silicone donut pan for this recipe.

PREP TIME: 15 minutes   **COOK TIME:** 15 minutes   **TOTAL TIME:** 30 minutes   **SERVES:** 6

RECIPE INGREDIENTS

- ✓ 1 1/4 c almond flour (125g)
- ✓ 1/3 c granulated erythritol (60g)
- ✓ 1 tsp baking powder
- ✓ 1/4 tsp xanthan gum
- ✓ 1/8 tsp salt
- ✓ 2 eggs room temperature
- ✓ 2 tbsp coconut oil melted
- ✓ 2 tbsp unsweetened almond milk
- ✓ 1/2 tsp vanilla extract
- ✓ 1/4 tsp liquid stevia

CINNAMON SUGAR COATING

- ✓ 4 tbsp granulated erythritol
- ✓ 1 1/2 tsp cinnamon

INSTRUCTIONS

01. In a large bowl, whisk together almond flour, erythritol, baking powder, xanthan gum, and salt.

02. In a medium bowl, lightly beat the room temperature eggs. Whisk in the melted coconut oil, almond milk, vanilla, and liquid stevia. Pour mixture into the bowl with dry ingredients and stir to combine.

03. Preheat air fryer at 330°F/165°C for 3 minutes. Spray donut pans or molds with avocado oil.

04. Pipe batter into six 3-inch donut cavities, filling about 3/4 full. Tap pan on counter to settle batter and reduce air bubbles.

05. Bake donuts at 330°F/165°C for 8 minutes. Check with toothpick for doneness. (With many air fryers, you may need to bake a set of 4 donuts first, then the remaining 2.)

06. Remove donuts from air fryer and let cool in pan for 5 minutes. Meanwhile, mix together the erythritol and cinnamon in a bowl.

07. After cooling time, carefully remove donuts from pan and coat both sides of each donut with cinnamon sugar mix.

08. Place coated donuts in air fryer with the flatter side down. Bake at 350°F/176°C for 2 minutes, immediately coat with cinnamon sugar for a final time. Enjoy!

Pumpkin Donuts

Enjoy this delicious fall favorite in the air fryer.
These pumpkin donuts taste of all things nice and pumpkin spice!
Note: You will need an air fryer silicone donut pan for this recipe.

PREP TIME: 15 minutes   **COOK TIME:** 10 minutes   **TOTAL TIME:** 25 minutes   **SERVES:** 6

RECIPE INGREDIENTS

DONUTS

- 1 3/4 c flour
- 1 tsp baking powder
- 1 tsp baking soda
- 1/2 tsp salt
- 1 1/2 tsp ground cinnamon
- 1 tsp pumpkin pie spice
- 1/2 c avocado oil (or melted coconut oil)
- 3/4 c packed light or dark brown sugar
- 2 large eggs, at room temperature
- 1 c canned pure pumpkin puree
- 1/3 c milk
- 1 tsp pure vanilla extract

ICING

- 3/4 c packed light or dark brown sugar
- 1/4 c milk
- 1 tbsp unsalted butter
- 1/2 tsp pure vanilla extract
- 1 1/2 c sifted confectioners sugar
- pinch of salt

INSTRUCTIONS

DONUTS

01. Whisk the flour, baking powder, baking soda, salt, cinnamon, and pumpkin pie spice together in a large bowl until combined. Set aside.

02. In a medium bowl, whisk the oil, brown sugar, eggs, pumpkin puree, milk, and vanilla extract together until combined.

03. Pour the wet ingredients into the dry ingredients, then fold everything together gently just until combined and no flour pockets remain.

04. Pipe or spoon batter in 3-inch silicone donut mold.

05. Preheat air fryer at 400°F/200°C for 2-3 minutes. Place donut mold in air fryer and bake at 330°F/165°C for 6-8 minutes, or until internal temperature of donuts reads above 160°F/71°C.

06. Make the icing, see below

07. Remove from air fryer and let cool for 2 minutes in mold, then carefully remove donuts from the mold.

08. Dip the tops of the pumpkin donuts into the icing. Place dipped donuts, dipped side up on a wire rack placed on a baking sheet so any excess icing can drip off. Top with chopped nuts or other toppings if desired. If applied lightly, the icing will eventually set in about 1 hour so you can stack or transport the donuts.

09. Cover leftover donuts tightly and store at room temperature for 1-2 days or in the refrigerator for up to 1 week.

ICING

01 Combine the brown sugar, milk, and butter in a medium saucepan over medium heat.

02 Stir until the butter has melted and mixture is smooth. Bring to a simmer. Allow to simmer for 1 minute then remove from heat and whisk in the vanilla extract and sifted confectioners' sugar until smooth and combined.

03 Taste, then add a pinch of salt if desired. I always add a tiny pinch.

04 Let the icing cool for 5-10 minutes to slightly thicken.

Pumpkin Chocolate Chip Muffins

*These pumpkin chocolate chip muffins are quick
and tasty treats that you can make during fall!*

PREP TIME: 20 minutes   **COOK TIME:** 15 minutes   **TOTAL TIME:** 35 minutes   **SERVES:** 24

RECIPE INGREDIENTS

- 3 large eggs
- 15 ounces pumpkin puree
- 1/2 c oil neutral flavored such as canola, vegetable, or avocado
- 1/2 c no-sugar added applesauce
- 1 c granulated sugar (7.5 ounces)
- 2 1/2 c all-purpose flour (12.5 ounces)
- 2 teaspoons pumpkin pie spice
- 1 teaspoon baking soda
- 1/2 teaspoon baking powder
- 1/2 teaspoon salt
- chocolate chips to taste

INSTRUCTIONS

01 In a large bowl, whisk together the wet ingredients. The eggs, pumpkin, oil, applesauce and sugar.

02 In a separate bowl, stir together dry ingredients. The flour, pumpkin pie spice, baking soda, baking powder and salt.

03 Add the dry ingredients to the wet ingredients. Mix until just combined and add in the chocolate chips to taste (don't overmix or the muffins may be dense and kind of heavy).

04 Place up to 9 silicone muffin liners in the air fryer basket. Lightly spray the liners with oil. Add muffin batter to the liners, about 3/4 of the way full.

05 Bake in the air fryer at 330°F/165°C for 13-15 minutes or until the internal temperature of the muffins reach 200°F/93°C.

06 Carefully remove from the air fryer basket. Let cool slightly then remove from the liner.

07 Repeat with the remaining batter. (I did this in 3 batches total).

15 Minute Cinnamon Rolls

Whip up some quick cinnamon rolls as a fun snack or treat!
Super easy with this 3-ingredient dough!

PREP TIME: 15 minutes   **COOK TIME:** 10 minutes   **TOTAL TIME:** 25 minutes   **SERVES:** 6

RECIPE INGREDIENTS

DOUGH

- 1 c self-rising flour
- 5 tbsp milk or 1/4 cup + 1 tbsp
- 3 tbsp butter melted

FILLING

- 1/4 c brown sugar
- 1/2 tbsp cinnamon
- 1/2 tbsp cornstarch
- 2 tbsp butter melted

ICING

- 1 oz cream cheese softened
- 2 tbsp powdered sugar
- 1/4 tsp vanilla
- 1/2 tbsp milk

INSTRUCTIONS

01. In a medium bowl, mix together the self-rising flour and milk until dough is just starting to come together. Add the melted butter and mix until combined. May need to use hands to finish mixing. Dough should be soft and smooth, like playdough.

02. In a small bowl, whisk together the brown sugar, cinnamon, cornstarch, and melted butter. Set aside.

03. Lightly flour or oil a flat surface. Roll dough into rectangle shape, between 1/8- and 1/4-inch thick, and about 12 inches by 8 inches. Spread filling over dough, leaving some space on the long edges. Roll dough up tightly, starting with long edge. Lightly pinch edge to seal. Cut into 9 rolls, each about 1 to 1 1/2 inches thick.

04. Oil your air fryer basket or use parchment paper. Lightly press down on the tops of each roll. Place rolls in the air fryer. Cook at 350°F/176°C for 5 minutes.

05. Meanwhile, beat together cream cheese, powdered sugar, vanilla, and milk for the icing.

06. Pipe or spread the icing over the tops of the warm rolls. Best served warm and fresh. Enjoy!

Molten Lava Cake

You won't believe how quick and easy this delicious chocolate molten lava air fryer cake recipe is! Enjoy for a special occasion or just a special treat!

PREP TIME: 12 minutes   **COOK TIME:** 10 minutes   **TOTAL TIME:** 22 minutes   **SERVES:** 6

RECIPE INGREDIENTS

- ✓ 8 oz Ghirardelli bittersweet 60% cacao chocolate baking bar
- ✓ 10 tbsp unsalted butter
- ✓ 1/2 tsp salt
- ✓ 1 1/2 c powdered sugar
- ✓ 1/2 c all-purpose flour
- ✓ 3 large eggs
- ✓ 3 egg yolks

RECIPE NOTES

If using salted butter, decrease salt to 1/4 tsp.

INSTRUCTIONS

01 Grease or spray six oven-safe 6 oz ramekins.

02 Break the chocolate bars into pieces. Combine chocolate and butter in a microwave-safe bowl and heat at half power for about 1 1/2 minutes, stirring about every 30 seconds, until smooth. Or melt in a double boiler over simmering water.

03 Add salt, powdered sugar, and flour. Stir well to combine. Mixture will be very thick, like cookie dough.

04 Add eggs and egg yolks and whisk until well combined. Batter will be fudgy and thick, but pourable.

05 Divide batter evenly among ramekins. Place as many as fit in your air fryer into the air fryer basket.

06 Cook at 400°F/200°C in the air fryer for about 8-10 minutes. 8 minutes for more fluid center and 10 for firmer. Top of cakes will look cakey with cracks and darker edges. Allow to set for 2 minutes. **The ramekins will be hot!**

07 Run a knife around the edge to loosen cakes. Invert onto a plate and tap the bottom of ramekin to help release cake. May need to gently wiggle it a little. Don't skip the tapping or part of your cake may stick to the ramekin.

08 Serve warm garnished with powdered sugar, berries, whipped cream, or ice cream.

Cinnamon Roll Twists

Cinnamon twists in the air fryer are the best quick, and not-so-healthy
snack or midnight treat. I personally prefer the taste of
Annie's packaged Cinnamon Rolls, but this will work with any brand!

PREP TIME: 15 minutes   **COOK TIME:** 12 minutes   **TOTAL TIME:** 27 minutes   **SERVES:** 6

RECIPE INGREDIENTS

- 1 package Annie's Cinnamon Rolls, 5 pack (or other giant sized refrigerator brand)

INSTRUCTIONS

01 Open the cinnamon roll package and take the rolls out.

02 Unroll the cinnamon rolls.

03 Join the two ends of the cinnamon dough together and twist the dough.

04 Lay each of the cinnamon twists on a piece of parchment paper in the air fryer basket.

05 Cook at 320°F/160°C for 12 minutes. Carefully flip the cinnamon twists at the halfway point.

06 Remove from the air fryer basket, top with icing, and enjoy!

Two-Ingredient Lava Cakes

Need a quick treat that will hit the spot? Make these
simple two-ingredient air fryer lava cakes in just 10 minutes!

PREP TIME: 3 minutes   **COOK TIME:** 7 minutes   **TOTAL TIME:** 10 minutes   **SERVES:** 4

RECIPE INGREDIENTS

- 1 package of your favorite cookie dough (I prefer Loren's)
- 1 baking chocolate bar

INSTRUCTIONS

01 Place a flattened cookie dough on the bottom of a lightly greased 8 oz ramekin.

02 Place 1 square of baking chocolate over the top of the cookie dough.

03 Then place one more layer of another flattened cookie dough.

04 Place the ramekins in the air fryer basket. Cook at 320°F/160°C for 7 minutes.

05 Let cool for 5-10 minutes and enjoy it topped with ice cream.

Apple Cobbler

Enjoy this indulgent fall apple cobbler dessert with whip cream or vanilla ice cream.

PREP TIME: 12 minutes   **COOK TIME:** 28 minutes   **TOTAL TIME:** 40 minutes   **SERVES:** 4

RECIPE INGREDIENTS

- 4 tart apples peeled, cored, and cut into chunks
- 1/2 tbsp lemon juice, freshly squeezed or bottled
- 1/4 tsp vanilla
- 1/4 c all-purpose flour or whole wheat flour
- 1/2 c rolled oats
- 1/2 c brown sugar
- 1/4 tsp ground cinnamon
- 4 tbsp butter softened to room temperature (1/2 stick of butter)

INSTRUCTIONS

01. In a medium bowl, toss the apples with the lemon juice and vanilla. Place the apples into a cake barrel accessory pan, spreading evenly to the edges. The apples can overlap.

02. In a different medium bowl stir together the flour, oats, brown sugar and cinnamon. Using a pastry blender, two forks or a whisk, mix the butter into dry ingredients until lumpy and coarsely mixed. Most of the dry ingredients should be incorporated with the butter to form large crumbs.

03. Sprinkle the mixture evenly over the apples.

04. Cover with foil, tucking it well under the pan and bake in an air fryer at 340°F/170°C for 20 minutes.

05. Remove foil and bake for another 8 minutes to create a crispy top layer.

RECIPE NOTES

I used 2 Granny Smith and 2 Honeycrisp. Firm, tart and sweet apples work the best for apple crisp. Feel free to experiment with different varieties.

The apples remain somewhat firm in the air fryer, yet soft enough to enjoy. So if you like a slightly softer apple base, then cook for an additional 5 minutes prior to removing the foil.

Mini Cheesecakes

*Creamy, simple, and full of rich flavor, this mini cheesecake
recipe is not only easier in the air fryer, but more delicious too!*

PREP TIME: 30 minutes   **COOK & REST TIME:** 145 minutes   **TOTAL TIME:** 175 minutes   **SERVES:** 4

RECIPE INGREDIENTS

CRUST

- ✔ 4 1/2 large rectangular graham crackers, crushed around 1 1/2 c
- ✔ 1 tbsp sugar
- ✔ 3 tbsp butter melted

CHEESECAKE CUSTARD

- ✔ 4 oz cream cheese softened at room temperature (make sure it is soft)
- ✔ 2 tbsp + 2 tsp
- ✔ 1/2 tsp vanilla extract
- ✔ 1 large egg room temperature
- ✔ 1 lemon, finely grated zest only

BLUEBERRY TOPPING

- ✔ 1 c blueberries rinsed
- ✔ 1/4 c water
- ✔ 2 tbsp + 2 tsp sugar
- ✔ 3/4 tbsp cornstarch mixed with 1 tbsp cold water

INSTRUCTIONS

01 **Make the crust.** In a small bowl, combine the crushed graham crackers, sugar, and butter until combined.

02 Place about 1/4 cup of the mixture into a ramekin (4 ramekins total). Using the bottom of a small cup, press down on the crust until flat.

03 Place in the air fryer basket and cook at 320°F/160°C for 6 minutes, or until very lightly browned. Remove from the air fryer basket and let it cool completely before adding the filling.

04 **Make the cheese custard.** In a medium bowl, combine the cream cheese, sugar, and vanilla and beat until thoroughly mixed and smooth. Add the eggs and beat well. Stir in the lemon zest. Pour into the cooled shell and cook for 15 minutes at 310°F/155°C. Cheesecake should be firm, it will be done when it reaches an internal temperature of 150°F/67°C. Let cool completely; about 1 hour.

05 **Make the blueberry topping.** While the custard is baking, combine the berries, water, and sugar in a medium saucepan and bring to a boil. Reduce the heat and simmer, covered, for 5 minutes, stirring once or twice to prevent sticking. Remove from the heat and add the cornstarch mixture. Return to a boil and cook for one minute, stirring constantly, until the mixture is thickened. Remove from the heat and cool until tepid.

06 Spoon the berries over the custard. Chill for at least one hour before serving. Enjoy!

Chewy Chocolate Chip Cookies

I love these air fryer chocolate chip cookies!
Perfectly baked, delicious flavor and texture, and no need to warm up the oven!

PREP TIME: 15 minutes   **COOK TIME:** 7 minutes   **TOTAL TIME:** 22 minutes   **SERVES:** 18

RECIPE INGREDIENTS

- 8 tbsp butter, room temperature
- 1/3 c granulated sugar
- 1/3 c brown sugar
- 1 large egg, room temperature
- 1 tsp vanilla
- 1/8 tsp lemon juice
- 1 c + 2 tbsp all-purpose flour
- 1/2 c old fashioned rolled oats
- 1/2 tsp baking soda
- 1/2 tsp salt
- 1/4 tsp cinnamon
- 1-1 1/2 c chocolate chips

INSTRUCTIONS

01. In a large bowl, cream together butter and sugars, until well blended. Mix in egg, vanilla, and lemon juice, blend until light and fluffy.

02. In a small bowl, combine flour, oats, baking soda, salt and cinnamon. Add to the large bowl and mix for about 45 seconds to combine. Don't overmix. Stir in chocolate chips with a spoon or spatula.

03. Line air fryer basket with heavy duty foil, leaving space at the top and bottom edges of the basket for air flow. Scoop cookie dough in balls (about 2 tbsp) and place on foil, leaving 1 1/2 to 2 inches between cookie dough balls. Lightly press the cookie dough down to flatten the tops of the cookies.

04. Air fry at 300°F/150°C for 6-8 minutes.

05. Lift foil and cookies out of the air fryer. Let cookies cool for about 5 minutes before transferring them to a cooling rack for another 5-10 minutes of cooling. If you handle the cookies too soon, they will fall apart.

Cake Mix Cookies

These tasty cake mix cookies are a simple treat thanks to your air fryer.
Enjoy fresh cookies for yourself or for a crowd in minutes!

PREP TIME: 7 minutes   **COOK TIME:** 4 minutes   **TOTAL TIME:** 11 minutes   **SERVES:** 12

RECIPE INGREDIENTS

- 1 devils food boxed cake mix
- 1/2 c unsweetened applesauce or avocado oil
- 2 large eggs
- 3/4 c chocolate chips or M&M style candy, optional
- 1/2 c sprinkles or nuts, optional

RECIPE NOTES

If your dough is too soft or runny, add about a 1/4 cup of flour. It is possible that with certain flavors, the cookies are not as thick and spread more.

INSTRUCTIONS

01 Place a piece of air fryer parchment paper in the bottom of the air fryer basket.

02 In a large mixing bowl, combine the cake mix, applesauce or oil, and eggs. Mix together until all of the ingredients are combined. The dough should be thick.

03 If using baking chips, candies, sprinkles, or nuts, stir them into the dough until they are evenly distributed.

04 Use a small scoop or spoon and drop scoops of dough into the prepared basket of your air fryer. Be sure to allow room for the dough to slightly spread. You will need to work in batches. Do not let the dough touch or overlap.

05 Cook at 370°F/187°C for 4 minutes per batch.

Scrumptious Nutella Bites

These air fryer Nutella bites are gooey, warm, and fluffy - in fact they could be called dangerously easy!

PREP TIME: 7 minutes   **COOK TIME:** 8 minutes   **TOTAL TIME:** 15 minutes   **SERVES:** 8

RECIPE INGREDIENTS

- ✓ 1 large egg
- ✓ 1 tbsp water
- ✓ 1 container refrigerated large flaky layer biscuits (16.3 oz, 8 count)
- ✓ 1/2 c Nutella
- ✓ powdered sugar, if desired

INSTRUCTIONS

01. Whisk egg with water.

02. Lightly flour surface and roll each biscuit to about a 5 inch diameter circle.

03. Brush flattened biscuit lightly with egg, making sure to brush all the way to the edges.

04. Cut each circle into 4 equal pieces.

05. Place 1/2 tsp Nutella in the middle of each piece of biscuit.

06. Fold biscuit piece in half over Nutella and firmly pinch shut.

07. Place biscuit pieces in a single layer in air fryer.

08. Cook for 7-8 minutes at 300°F/150°C until golden brown, flip biscuits halfway through cooking.

09. Dust with powdered sugar.

10. Best served warm.

How to Make S'mores

Enjoy tasty and melty s'mores anytime of the year in your air fryer!

PREP TIME: 2 minutes   **COOK TIME:** 10 minutes   **TOTAL TIME:** 12 minutes   **SERVES:** 4

RECIPE INGREDIENTS

- 4 Graham Crackers broken in half
- 4 marshmallows
- 1 milk chocolate Hershey's bar divided in 4

RECIPE NOTES

Cooking time may vary considerably depending on your air fryer model. A toaster oven air fryer can roast mallows in as little as 30 seconds. But most standard air fryer models take at least 5 minutes. I would highly recommend peeking at your s'mores starting at the 3 minute mark.

INSTRUCTIONS

01 Place four graham cracker halves inside the air fryer basket.

02 Cut a small slice off the bottom of each marshmallow, and stick it to the graham cracker. This will keep it secure during cooking.

03 Cook at 370°F/187°C for about 7-8 minutes, or until the marshmallow is golden brown.

04 Add the desired amount of Hershey's chocolate and top with the other graham cracker.

05 Place back in the air fryer for another 2 minutes or until the chocolate begins to melt.

S'mores Dip

*Enjoy the delights of summer any time of the year with
this simple and easy s'mores dip.*

PREP TIME: 2 minutes   **COOK TIME:** 6 minutes   **TOTAL TIME:** 8 minutes   **SERVES:** 2

RECIPE INGREDIENTS

- 3/4 c chocolate chips
- 18-20 marshmallows
- 1 bag graham crackers

INSTRUCTIONS

01. Place parchment paper in a 7" air fryer pan or spring form pan. (It's not necessary to use parchment paper, it just makes cleaning up easier.)

02. Layer 1/2 cup of chocolate chips, then marshmallows, then more chocolate chips inside the pan.

03. Sprinkle broken graham crackers over top.

04. Cook at 350°F/176°C for 4-6 minutes.

05. Serve warm with graham crackers or apples.

The Very Best Pumpkin Pie Cake Bars

PREP TIME: 20 minutes   **COOK TIME:** 20 minutes   **TOTAL TIME:** 40 minutes   **SERVES:** 4

RECIPE INGREDIENTS

- 215 grams yellow cake mix (half a box of cake mix)
- 1/4 c butter melted and cooled
- 1 1/2 large eggs, divided
- 7 1/2 oz pure pumpkin puree
- 1/3 c milk

TOPPING

- 2 tbsp sugar
- 2 tbsp butter room temperature
- 1/2 tsp cinnamon
- whipped cream for serving

INSTRUCTIONS

01. From the half box of the cake mix, take out 1/2 cup and set aside in a bowl for the topping, for later.

02. With the remaining cake mix, add a 1/4 cup of melted butter, and 1/2 an egg (see notes). Mix together until combined.

03. Lightly spray the bottom of a 7-inch springform pan (or a different dish that will fit in your air fryer. A cake barrel or cake pan also works).

04. Spread the batter in the bottom of the pan. Cook in the air fryer for 320°F/160°C for 10 minutes.

05. In a bowl, mix together the pumpkin puree, 1/3 cup milk, and 1 egg.

06. In a separate bowl, mix together the 1/2 cup of cake mix, with 2 tbsp of sugar, and 1/2 tsp of cinnamon. Then add in the butter and mix until crumbly with a fork.

07. Carefully remove the pan from the air fryer basket.

08. Add the pumpkin puree layer to the cake, then the crumble topping mixture.

09. To avoid the crumble mixture from blowing around in the air fryer, lightly spray the top of the cake with oil or cover with foil, tucking under bottom of pan and take foil off during the last couple of minutes.

OVEN INSTRUCTIONS

01 This recipe works great in the oven as well. Just double the called for ingredients. Be sure to set aside 1 cup of cake mix for the crumble topping.

02 Mix ingredients together as directed. Press the first layer into a lightly oiled 9x13 baking pan. Place the pumpkin layer next, and then finally the crumble on top. Cook for 45-50 minutes at 350°F/176°C, or until the middle is cooked all the way. A toothpick inserted in the middle will come out clean.

10 Cook in the air fryer at 320°F/160°C for another 10-15 minutes, or until the top is golden brown and the inside is cooked through.

11 Once cooled, remove from the springform pan and enjoy with whipped cream.

3 Ingredient Apple Fritters

*These tasty and easy 3 ingredient apple fritters
are our new go-to treat for any occasion!*

PREP TIME: 8 minutes   **COOK TIME:** 12 minutes   **TOTAL TIME:** 20 minutes   **SERVES:** 4

RECIPE INGREDIENTS

FOR THE FRITTERS

- ✔ 1 package of Pillsbury French bread dough
- ✔ 1/2 can of apple pie filling, about 2/3 c
- ✔ 1 tbsp ground cinnamon
- ✔ Avocado oil spray

GLAZE INGREDIENTS

- ✔ 1/4 c butter or 1/2 a stick
- ✔ 1/2 tsp vanilla
- ✔ 1 tbsp cream or milk
- ✔ 1 c powdered sugar

GLAZE INSTRUCTIONS

01. Place butter in a small saucepan over medium-high heat. Continue melting the butter until it starts to foam and turn brown. Once browned, remove from heat to cool slightly. You should smell a nutty aroma and see brown specks in the butter. Do not let it burn.

02. Place powdered sugar in a small bowl. Add browned butter, milk and vanilla whisking until smooth. (If the mixture is too thin for your liking, simply add more powdered sugar.) Set aside.

INSTRUCTIONS

01. Preheat the air fryer at 400°F/200°C for 5 minutes.

02. On a cutting board, cut up the Pillsbury dough into bite size pieces using a bench scraper (the pieces can be larger or smaller).

03. Keep the dough on the cutting board and add the cinnamon and about 2/3 cup of apple pie filling to the dough.

04. Using a bench scraper, mix the dough, filling, and cinnamon together.

05. Form the mixture into a log. You may need to use flour to prevent the dough mixture sticking to the counter.

06. Cut the log into 8 pieces.

07. Place a piece of parchment paper inside the air fryer basket and spray the paper with oil.

08. Place the fritters inside the basket.

09. Spray the fritters with avocado oil.

10. Cook at 350°F/176°C for 12 minutes.

11. At the 9 minute mark, turn the fritters over to brown the bottoms.

12. When the fritters are finished, dip the top in the glaze and let it drip down.

Puff Pastry Danishes

Ready in minutes with your air fryer,
these cute Danishes will be a new family favorite!

PREP TIME: 15 minutes   **COOK TIME:** 10 minutes   **TOTAL TIME:** 25 minutes   **SERVES:** 9

RECIPE INGREDIENTS

- 8 oz package cream cheese, softened to room temperature
- 1/4 c sugar
- 2 tbsp flour
- 1/2 tsp vanilla extract
- 2 large egg yolks
- 1 tbsp water
- 17.3 oz package frozen puff pastry, thawed
- 2/3 c seedless raspberry jam or jam of choice

INSTRUCTIONS

01. Beat cream cheese, sugar, flour, and vanilla until smooth.

02. Beat in 1 egg yolk.

03. On a lightly floured surface, unfold each sheet of puff pastry and cut each into nine squares. Or roll pastry until about 1/8" to 1/4" thick.

04. Next make the egg wash by mixing together 1 tbsp water and 1 egg yolk.

05. Top each pastry square with about 1 tbsp of cream cheese mixture & 1 rounded tsp jam

06. Bring 2 opposite corners of pastry over filling, sealing with yolk mixture.

07. Brush tops with remaining yolk mixture.

08. In batches, place in a single layer on lightly greased tray in air fryer basket.

09. Cook at 320°F/160°C for 8-10 minutes until golden brown, no need to flip.

10. Serve warm & refrigerate leftovers

Delicious Fried Oreos

*You can't go wrong with this easy, quick air fryer fried Oreos recipe.
They are a big hit with our friends and family!*

PREP TIME: 5 minutes   **COOK TIME:** 5 minutes   **TOTAL TIME:** 10 minutes   **SERVES:** 9

RECIPE INGREDIENTS

- ✓ 1 can refrigerator crescent roll dough original size 8 rolls package
- ✓ 9 Oreo cookies

RECIPE NOTES

Any cream filled cookie will work for these tasty morsels

INSTRUCTIONS

01. Unroll the crescent roll dough onto counter.

02. Place a cookie on the wide end and wrap each cookie entirely in a single layer of dough. Pinch off excess dough, remove it and use for wrapping the ninth cookie.

03. Place in air fryer basket and cook at 350°F/176°C for 4-5 minutes, until golden brown. Turn and cook 1-2 minutes more if bottoms are not cooked fully.

04. Immediately remove from air fryer and dust with powdered sugar. Enjoy while warm!

05. If needed, reheat by air frying at 350°F/176°C for 2-3 minutes.

Peanut Butter Cups

Tasty and crazy easy, this delicious and simple air fryer treat is perfect for peanut butter chocolate lovers. Plus, it's way healthier than deep frying!

PREP TIME: 10 minutes   **COOK TIME:** 6 minutes   **TOTAL TIME:** 16 minutes   **SERVES:** 6

RECIPE INGREDIENTS

- 12 chilled peanut butter cups
- 1 can crescent roll dough

INSTRUCTIONS

01. Chill the peanut butter cups for at least 1 hour. (If you are in a rush, you can skip this step and they will still taste fine or place in freezer for 10 minutes).

02. Roll out crescent roll dough and seal seams.

03. Place 12 peanut butter cups evenly spaced out on dough.

04. Cut the dough into squares and wrap around each peanut butter cup.

05. Cook at 380°F/193°C for 6 minutes, flipping at the halfway point.

06. Enjoy!

Churros with Chocolate Dipping Sauce

No need to deep fry churros if you have an air fryer and this air fryer churros recipe! So delicious and easy!

PREP TIME: 20 minutes   **COOK TIME:** 8 minutes   **TOTAL TIME:** 28 minutes   **SERVES:** 8

RECIPE INGREDIENTS

- 1 c water
- 1/3 c unsalted butter cut into cubes
- 2 tbsp sugar
- 1/4 tsp salt
- 1 c all-purpose flour
- 2 large eggs
- 1 tsp vanilla
- oil spray

CINNAMON-SUGAR COATING

- 1/4 c sugar
- 1/2 tsp cinnamon

RECIPE NOTES

Chocolate Dipping Sauce: Add 6 tbsp chocolate chips and 1/4 cup heavy cream to a microwave-safe bowl. Microwave in 30-second increments, stirring in between, until smooth.

INSTRUCTIONS

01. Prepare a baking sheet with a silicone baking mat or parchment paper, spray with oil spray.

02. In a medium saucepan over medium-high heat, combine water, butter, sugar, and salt. Bring to a boil.

03. Reduce heat to medium-low, add flour all at once and stir constantly until the dough comes together, starts to leave the sides of the pan and is smooth. Transfer dough to a mixing bowl. Let cool for 4 minutes.

04. Add eggs and vanilla and mix with an electric mixer until dough comes together. It will look kind of like thick, sticky mashed potatoes. Transfer dough to a piping bag fitted with a large star tip (like Wilton 1M).

05. Pipe dough onto the prepared baking sheet in 4-inch lengths, cutting the end with scissors. Then refrigerate for 30 minutes, or up to an hour.

06. Carefully transfer churros with a cookie spatula to the air fryer basket, leaving about 1/2 inch between churros. Spray churros with oil spray.

07. Cook at 380°F/193°C for 8-10 minutes, until golden brown (cooking time may vary depending on the air fryer).

08. In a shallow bowl, combine the sugar and cinnamon. Immediately after cooking, transfer the churros into the cinnamon-sugar mixture and roll or toss to coat. Serve fresh and warm.

Dessert Hand Pies

*There are so many ways to fill your dessert hand pies! Pick out one or
two of the different fillings to try and decide which one you like the best!*

PREP TIME: 20 minutes   **COOK TIME:** 8 minutes   **TOTAL TIME:** 28 minutes   **SERVES:** 14

RECIPE INGREDIENTS

- 2, 9" pie crusts
- egg wash

FOR HOMEMADE APPLE PIE FILLING

- 2-3 fresh apples
- 2 tbsp lemon juice or to your taste
- 3/4 c water or apple juice
- 1 1/2 tbsp unsalted butter
- 1/4 c sugar, white or brown
- 1/4 tsp salt
- 2 tbsp cornstarch
- 2 tbsp cold water

RECIPE NOTES

You can use any fruit for the pie filling. You will want roughly 2 cups or 16 ounces of fruit. You can use fresh or frozen. If you are using frozen fruit, you don't need to thaw it beforehand. Use water or a juice that compliments the flavor of the fruit you are using.

INSTRUCTIONS

01. Chop the apples into bite size cubes or smaller.

02. Add the apples and butter in a large saucepan over medium-high heat until the butter is melted and bubbling.

03. Add the water (or apple juice), sugar, lemon juice, and salt and mix until combined. Bring to a simmer.

04. Mix together the cornstarch with the water to make a slurry - it should be like a creamy paste.

05. Once the apple mixture is simmering, add the cornstarch and cook for a couple of minutes until the mixture is clear and has thickened.

06. Once thick, remove the saucepan from the heat and let it cool completely.

07. While the mixture cools, cut each of the pie crusts into seven, 3.5" circles (14 small crusts total).

08. Once the mixture has cooled, add about 1-2 tablespoons of apple pie filling in each pie crust circle. Fold in half and seal the top and bottom crusts together with water. Then close shut with a fork. Spread an egg wash over the top, if desired, or spritz with oil.

09. Place in the air fryer basket and cook at 350°F/176°C for 6-8 minutes, or until the pie crusts are golden brown.

S'mores Hand Pies

RECIPE INGREDIENTS

- ✓ 2, 9" pie crusts
- ✓ egg wash

FOR FILLING

- ✓ 2 Hershey's chocolate bars
- ✓ 1 c miniature marshmallows
- ✓ 3 rectangles Crushed graham cracker

INSTRUCTIONS

01. Cut each of the pie crusts into seven, 3.5" circles (14 small crusts total).

02. Assemble the hand pies by placing three small Hershey's chocolate bar squares on each circle. Add about 6 miniature marshmallows on top of the chocolate on each pie. Seal the top and bottom crusts together with water and then seal with a fork. Spread an egg wash over the top and then some crushed graham crackers if desired. Cook at 350°F/175°C for 6-8 minutes.

Tasty Lemon Hand Pies

RECIPE INGREDIENTS

- ✓ 2, 9" pie crusts
- ✓ egg wash

FOR FILLING

- ✓ 1/2 c sugar
- ✓ 2 large eggs
- ✓ 1 lemon zested
- ✓ 1/2 c lemon juice
- ✓ 1/4 c melted butter

INSTRUCTIONS

01. Cut each of the pie crusts into seven, 3.5" circles (14 small crusts total).

02. In a bowl, combine sugar and eggs. Whisk in lemon zest and lemon juice. Stir in melted butter. Microwave lemon mixture for 1 minute, then stir. Continue to heat lemon mixture in 1-minute intervals until mixture begins to thicken and easily coats the back of a spoon. Refrigerate to set.

03. Place 1-2 tablespoons of pie filling in each pie crust circle. Seal the top and bottom crusts together with water and then seal with a fork. Spread an egg wash over the top. Cook at 350°F/176°C for 6-8 minutes.

Peach Hand Pies

RECIPE INGREDIENTS

- ✅ 2, 9" pie crusts
- ✅ egg wash

FOR FILLING

- ✅ 1 can (21 oz) peach pie filling
- ✅ cinnamon to taste (if using an entire can about 1 tsp cinnamon)

GLAZE

- ✅ 2 1/2 c powdered sugar
- ✅ 1/4 c milk

INSTRUCTIONS

01 Mix together pie filling with cinnamon in a bowl. Make sure that the peaches are in bite-sized cubes or smaller.

02 Place about 1-2 tbsp of pie filling in each pie crust circle. Seal the top and bottom crusts together with water and then seal with a fork. Spread an egg wash over the top. Cook at 350°F/176°C for 6-8 minutes.

03 Beat together glaze ingredients while cooking. Remove hand pies from the air fryer basket and drop into the glaze while warm. Cover completely. Place on parchment paper and allow to cool for at least 5 minutes.

Gingerbread Bites

*Air fryer gingerbread bites are a fun and simple dessert
that are best enjoyed during the holiday season.*

PREP TIME: 6 minutes   **COOK TIME:** 10 minutes   **TOTAL TIME:** 16 minutes   **SERVES:** 8

RECIPE INGREDIENTS

- ✓ 1 can crescent rolls
- ✓ 8 oz cream cheese
- ✓ 1 tbsp + 1/4-1/2 cup sugar divided
- ✓ 1/2 tbsp ground allspice
- ✓ 1/2 tbsp ground cinnamon
- ✓ 1/2 tbsp ground ginger
- ✓ 3/4 tsp ground cloves
- ✓ 3/4 tsp ground nutmeg

INSTRUCTIONS

01. Mix together all the spices plus 1/4-1/2 cup sugar (to your taste) in a medium bowl. Set aside.

02. Put the remaining 1 tbsp sugar and softened cream cheese in a small bowl. Use a fork to mash cream cheese until evenly combined.

03. Unroll crescent dough. Put about 1 tbsp of cream cheese mixture on the large end of crescent triangles.

04. Gently fold crescent dough to cover cream cheese. Gently press a round disc shape between your hands. Dip bites into spice mixture and press on both sides.

05. Place bites into a lightly sprayed air fryer basket on parchment paper.

06. Cook for 8 to 9 minutes at 350°F/176°C.

07. Remove and serve immediately. Enjoy!

Glazed Fresh Fruit

This fresh, light, and incredibly easy fruit recipe is the perfect side or snack during the summer. Or you can enjoy it for a tasty breakfast or dessert.

PREP TIME: 5 minutes   **COOK TIME:** 8 minutes   **TOTAL TIME:** 13 minutes   **SERVES:** 4

RECIPE INGREDIENTS

FRUIT *SEE NOTES

- 1 c fresh pineapple cut into bite sized pieces
- 1 c mango cut into bite sized pieces
- 1 c apricot chunks cut into bite sized pieces

GLAZE

- 1/2 c brown sugar
- 1/2 c orange juice
- 1/4 tsp cinnamon

RECIPE NOTES

Almost any fruit but melons will work. Use approximately 1 cup of each.

INSTRUCTIONS

01 Mix together the brown sugar, orange juice, and cinnamon until well combined.

02 Add the glaze to the fruit, coating thoroughly.

03 Preheat the air fryer to 390°F/398°C for 5 minutes.

04 Lightly spray the air fryer basket. Add the fruit to the basket, and cook for 4 minutes.

05 Give the fruit a stir. If you prefer a more tender texture, cook for an additional 4 minutes and spritz with oil if desired.

06 Carefully remove from the air fryer basket and enjoy!

07 **Optional:** top with coconut or chopped nuts.

Cupcakes

Did you know you can make cupcakes in the air fryer?
Savor cupcakes for a few people in minutes thanks to your air fryer.

PREP TIME: 10 minutes   **COOK TIME:** 11 minutes   **TOTAL TIME:** 21 minutes   **SERVES:** 12

RECIPE INGREDIENTS

- 1 box of cake mix

INSTRUCTIONS

01. Prepare the cake mix according to the package directions.

02. Place the batter into lightly greased silicone muffin liners.

03. Place in the air fryer basket and cook at 350°F/175°C for 11 minutes.

04. Remove from the air fryer basket, let the cupcakes cool, and top with your favorite frosting.

Grilled Peaches

Nothing says yummy like a fresh, grilled peach topped with ice cream. With your air fryer, you can enjoy this tasty treat anytime of day without turning on the grill! Note: You will need a Sear'NSizzle GrillGrate plate to cook these peaches to perfection.

PREP TIME: 5 minutes   **COOK TIME:** 6 minutes   **TOTAL TIME:** 11 minutes   **SERVES:** 2-4

RECIPE INGREDIENTS

- 1-2 peaches, ripe but firm
- 1-2 tbsp butter, melted
- 1-2 tbsp brown sugar, to taste
- cinnamon, to taste

INSTRUCTIONS

01. Place a Sear'NSizzle GrillGrate plate inside the air fryer. Preheat the air fryer at 400°F/200°C for 5 minutes.

02. Slice the peaches in half.

03. Brush with melted butter

04. Sprinkle with desired amount of brown sugar and cinnamon. Rub brown sugar and cinnamon into the peaches and place the flesh side down on the plate in the air fryer.

05. Cook at 370°F/185°C for 6 minutes. Top with ice cream if desired.

NOTES

NOTES

COOKING PREPACKAGED FROZEN FOODS

One of the great benefits of using an air fryer is how quickly it can cook your food. This is especially true when cooking frozen foods. As a general rule of thumb, you'll be cooking at higher temperatures (380-400ºF/190-200ºC) and cut the recommended oven cook time in half. Use this helpful little list to find the temperature and time for many favorite frozen foods.

- **Frozen Pizza:** 8 minutes at 400ºF/200ºC
- **Burritos:** 8 minutes at 400ºF/200ºC
- **Pizza Rolls:** 10 minutes at 380ºF/193ºC
- **Corn dogs:** 10 minutes at 370ºF/183ºC
- **French Fries:** 10-20 minutes at 380°F/193°C depending on thickness of the fries, shake halfway.
- **Hash Brown Patties:** 8-10 minutes 400°F/200°C
- **Breaded Shrimp:** 8 minutes at 400°F/200°C
- **Frozen WonTon:** 8 minutes at 350°F/175°C
- **Tempura Shrimp:** 7 minutes at 400°F/200°C
- **Bagel Bites:** remove from packaging 6-8 minutes at 380°F/193°C
- **Vegetable Spring Rolls:** 6-8 minutes at 370°F/185°C, flipping halfway
- **Eggo© or other Frozen Waffles or Pancakes:** 6-7 minutes at 380ºF/193ºC flipping halfway
- **Frozen Broccoli or Cauliflower:** 10 minutes at 300ºF/150ºC. If desired, lightly spray and season with your favorite seasonings, then cook at 400ºF/200ºC for 1-2 minutes more for a roasted effect.
- **Mixed Frozen Vegetables:** Cook at 350°F/175°C for 3 minutes to thaw, carefully pour out any excess liquid. Increase temperature to 400°F/200°C and cook for 6 minutes.
- **Chicken Nuggets:** 6-8 minutes at 380°F/193°C flipping/shaking halfway.
- **Chicken Taquitos:** 8 minutes at 400°F/200°C, rotating halfway.
- **Impossible Burger:** 10-12 minutes at 370°F/185°C, flipping halfway.
- **Johnsonville Sausage Strips:** 5 minutes at 400°F/200°C.
- **Mandarin Orange Chicken:** Cook in the air fryer at 350°F/175°C for 15 minutes. Add frozen broccoli at the halfway point.

SUBSTITUTIONS AND
HOMEMADE SEASONINGS & SAUCES

Self Rising Flour Place 1/2 tsp salt, 1 1/2 tsp of baking powder in a dry measuring cup and add enough flour to make 1 cup.

Buttermilk Substitute Add 1 tsp lemon juice or vinegar into 1 c regular milk. Let stand 5 minutes and stir.

Homemade Honey Mustard Combine 2 tbsp of Dijon mustard, 2 tbsp of honey, and 1 tsp of mayonnaise

Taco Seasoning Mix

1 tbsp chili powder

1 1/2 tsp ground cumin

1 tsp salt

1/2 tsp black pepper

1/2 tsp paprika

1/4 tsp garlic powder

1/4 tsp onion powder

1/4 tsp dried oregano

pinch cayenne pepper

Creole Seasoning

2 tbsp onion powder

2 tbsp garlic powder

2 tbsp dried oregano

2 tbsp dried basil

1 tbsp dried thyme

1 tbsp ground black pepper

1 tbsp ground white pepper

1 tbsp cayenne pepper

5 tbsp paprika, (smoked if possible)

3 tbsp salt

Fajita Seasoning

2 tsp chili powder

1 tsp paprika, (smoked if possible)

1 tsp dried oregano

1 tsp salt

1 tsp sugar

1/2 tsp ground cumin

1/2 tsp garlic powder

1/2 tsp onion powder

1/4 tsp cayenne pepper

Ranch Seasoning

1/3 c dry powdered buttermilk

2 tbsp dried parsley

1 1/2 tsp dried dill weed

2 tsp garlic powder

2 tsp onion powder

2 tsp dried minced onion

1 tsp dried chives

1 tsp pepper

1 tsp salt

Fry Sauce

1/2 c mayonnaise (120 grams)

1/4 c ketchup (68 grams)

1 tbsp sugar

1 tbsp red wine vinegar

1/2 tsp worcestershire sauce

1/4 tsp salt

1/4 tsp paprika

1/4 tsp ground mustard

1/4 tsp onion powder

Sweet Baby Ray's BBQ Sauce Copycat Recipe

INGREDIENTS

- 1 1/4 c ketchup (340 grams)
- 1 c dark brown sugar
- 1/4 c molasses (60 grams)
- 1/4 c pineapple juice
- 1/4 c water
- 1 tbsp hickory liquid smoke
- 2 1/2 tsp ground mustard
- 2 tsp paprika
- 1/2 tsp garlic powder
- pinch cayenne pepper
- 1 1/2 tsp kosher salt
- 1 tsp black pepper

INSTRUCTION

1. Whisk together all ingredients in a medium pot over medium heat. Bring to a boil, then reduce heat and simmer for 5 minutes, until sugar has dissolved.

2. Simmer for up to 15 minutes, until desired thickness is reached. Keep in mind that it may thicken slightly more as it cools.

3. Serve immediately or cover and store in the refrigerator for up to a month.

US/METRIC CONVERSION CHARTS

US VOLUME MEASURE	METRIC EQUIVALENT
1/4 tsp	1.25 ml
1/3 tsp	1.65 ml
1/2 tsp	2.5 ml
1 tsp	5 ml
2 tsp	7 ml
1/2 tbsp (1 1/2 tsp)	7.5 ml
1 tbs (3 tsp)	15 ml
2 tbsp 1/8 c	30 ml
2 oz. 1/4 c	60 ml
4 oz. 1/2 c	120 ml
5.3 oz. 2/3 c	160 ml
6 oz. 3/4 c	180 ml
8 oz. 1 c	250 ml
12 oz. 1 1/2 c	375 ml
16 oz. 2 c	500 ml
36 oz. 1 quart	about 1 litre

TEMPERATURE CONVERSIONS			
Fahren-heit, (F)	Celsius, (C)	Gas Mark	Description
145	60		
165	70		
200	90		
250	120	.50	Very Slow
300	150	2	Slow
320	160	3	
340	170		
350	175	4	Moderate
360	182		
370	187	5	
380	193		
390	198		
400	204	6	Hot
450	230	8	Very Hot
500	260	10	Extremely Hot

RECOMMENDED INTERNAL TEMPERATURES OF MEATS AND BAKED GOODS

I always recommend using your instant read thermometer to make sure food is cooked properly (and to help you avoid overcooking and drying food out!). Food is done when it reaches these internal temperatures. I usually pull whole cuts of meat out about 3-5 degrees before before the internal temperature is reached. Because the meat will continue to cook as it rests. After 5 minutes of resting, you can double check the meat has come to temp.

MEATS	FAHRENHEIT	CELSIUS
Whole cuts of Pork, Beef, Veal, and Lamb		
Rare	120°– 125°	45° – 50°
Medium-Rare	130° – 135°	55° – 60°
Medium	140° – 145°	60° – 65°
Medium-Well	150° – 155°	65° – 70°
Well Done	160°	70°
Ground Meats (beef, veal, lamb, pork)	160°	70°
Poultry (chicken, ground chicken, turkey, etc.)	165°	75°
Fish & Shellfish	145°	65°
Eggs/Custards	160°	71°
BAKED GOODS		
Bread - crusty, yeast, sourdough	200° – 210°	95°
Bread - Enriched/ Sweet yeast	180° –190°	85°
Quick Breads/Muffins	190°	88°
Cake, cupcakes	205° – 209°	98°
Tres leches, Upside Down Cake, Scones	200°	98°
Molten Chocolate Cake	160°	71°
Pie –Single, Double fruit or meat	170°	77°
Pumpkin – Custard pie	175°	79°
Brownies – gooey	190° – 200°	87° – 93°
Brownies – cake	205° – 210°	96° – 99°
Cookies	170° – 180°	77° – 82°

NOTES

Made in the USA
Coppell, TX
17 December 2024

42966081R00144